A Pail of Beer

and Other Lessons Learned

Frederick Kenney

Floridafred LLC

Frederickkenney.com

ISBN: 979-8-9906792-3-8

Library of Congress Control Number: 2024938034

This book is dedicated to Chief George Atwell
(Grandpa George) who saved my life
and Detective lieutenant Gerald Colbert
(Uncle Jerry) who pointed me in the right direction.

Detective Lt. Gerald Colbert
"Uncle Jerry"

Chief of Police George Atwell
"Grandpa George"

Contents

Chapter 1

THE BEGINNING

My life began on Franklin Ave, in Mount Vernon, New York. I spent my first ten years in that environment, surrounded by countless cousins, aunts, uncles, grandmothers, grandfathers, and my mom. My grandmother, especially, who protected me and made me feel safe, was my angel. My family occupied three large old homes, which we referred to as the compound. A loving family surrounded me. I lived in a small room in my great-grandfather's house.

Absent, was my father, who abandoned us when I was an infant. This fostered a disquiet yet inquisitive attitude that I would carry forward. I recall the last time I did NOT see him. I was 5 or 6 years old. My mother dressed me and sent me outside to wait for him. It was not the first time, I can vaguely remember, but it was the last time. He did not show, and I never heard from him again. As the years passed, I begged my mother for information about him. She would never speak of him or answer any of my questions. If I pressed her, she would cry.

My cousin Ronnie was a couple of years older than I and he lived next door to us with his sister Nancy who was my age. Cousins Patty and Sue lived upstairs with their younger brother Harold. We were all close in age and interacted every day. There was a wide dirt driveway between the houses where we played ball and other games. We would go out into the woods and pick berries and apples. We might wind up in one of many kitchens where aunts or grandparents would kindly feed us.

The very first recollection of my life was when I was maybe six years old. It would take many years for me to understand fully what happened that day. We were playing "Hide and Go Seek". Ronnie was hiding his eyes and counting at the big tree in front. The rest of us ran off to hide. Even at that early stage in my life I was an overachiever. I was going to find the best hiding place. Alongside the large staircase leading to the main entrance there was two steps down leading to the basement entrance. Just past the basement entrance was a storage room. It was dirty and crammed with old furniture as I searched for the best place to hide. I found an old ice box, opened the door and climbed in. The door closed with a resounding clank as the latch on the outside functioned to ensure an airtight seal. It was a tight fit with my knees up against my chin and it was hard to breath. It only took a few seconds for me to realize I was locked in with no way to escape. I remember thinking I was going to get into trouble.

I could not have been inside for more than a few minutes when suddenly the door opened. It was my cousin Nancy who acted surprised to see me.

"Freddie, what are you doing in there," she said and then she ran off.

I climbed out of that death trap unharmed, never giving it another thought.

Years later, as I dealt with issues of PTSD related to my military service this incident returned to me in a dream. It struck me that my cousin Nancy had never received credit for saving my life. She most likely was not even aware how deadly that game may have been. I replayed the incident over and over in my mind. I felt like I was missing something. I could hear her words so clearly, "Freddie, what are you doing in there."

It finally came to me. While my cousin Nancy may have saved my life I in turn saved her life, and maybe that is why I was in there in the first place. Nancy wasn't looking for me, it was our turn to hide. She opened that door looking for the perfect place to hide herself. If I had not been there, I am sure she would have climbed in as I had. Who would have saved her?

Another early recollection was when my great grandfather was in his seventies, and I was about 7. He would sit in a big, stuffed chair by a window in the living room smoking a cigar. A small side table on his right held a glass into which he constantly dipped the end of his cigar before puffing on it. A cigar box that held a special interest for me was on the bottom shelf.

"Grandpa, can I play with the chips?" I would beg.

He would retrieve the cigar box and place it on the floor beside me. Inside the box were dazzling disks, which I would stack and unstack to hear the clinking sound they made. Years later, I would realize the glass he dipped his cigar into contained whiskey, and the dazzling chips were twenty-dollar gold pieces.

One day, my grandpa asked me to go to the corner and get him a pail of beer. The land around our compound was mostly woodland, containing wild berries, apple trees, and sometimes strange people. A couple hundred yards down our street, on the corner, was an apartment house with a bar at street level. Grandpa handed me a metal pail with a lid and five cents.

"Go get your grandpa a pail of beer."

I was afraid and told him I didn't want to go.

"Freddie, someday you'll be old like your grandpa, and you'll want someone to get you a pail of beer."

As a 7-year-old, I felt that was a pretty strong argument, so I agreed to go. Walking past the wooded area, I was afraid, but not nearly as afraid as I was when I entered the bar. It was dark and smelled of beer and cigars, plus whatever else was in the air. There were gruff voices and the clanging of glasses, but undeterred, I walked up to the bar, placing the pail and nickel up high onto the bar.

"My grandpa wants a pail of beer."

"Who's your grandpa?"

"Grandpa George," I said. "Up the street."

"George Atwell?" repeated the bartender.

With that, he filled up the pail and handed it down to me.

"Tell your grandpa the next time he wants a beer to come and get it himself."

When I told my mother about my adventure, she was furious. I could hear her yelling at my grandfather from my room. My mother forbade me from ever going to the bar again. It wasn't until I was 16 years old that I would again order a beer in a bar. I was big for my age.

Grandpa was always busy with one project or another, maintaining our homes. One day, when I was going to school, I had to leave by the basement door because Grandpa was painting the front steps. When I got home, the front steps were freshly painted green, and so was my basketball.

Before he passed from this earth, Grandpa would do me one last big favor. Grandpa was in his chair, and my mom was at work. I was running around a little more wild than usual. I ran down the hallway toward the front door at a speed that was much too fast.

As I ran into the door, I extended both hands to stop myself. The top half of the door contained a large pane of glass, and I put both arms through the glass, shattering it. I remember screaming at the sight of the blood gushing from my right wrist. I had severed just about everything in my wrist, and I was bleeding out. My uncle Jack drove, and Grandpa clenched my arm, bent tightly at the elbow. At some point, I passed out. At the hospital, the doctor performed a medical miracle, putting me back together. The doctor credited my survival to the swift action of my grandfather. I suffered no lasting complications, and my recovery was swift. My grandpa saved my life.

Grandpa George G. Atwell was born in Ireland on July 1, 1870. At the age of 19, he sold a cow to pay for passage to the United States. I discovered that fact in a letter that was written at the time of his travel. Within a few years of his arrival in the new country, he sent for his parents. While working in real estate, he purchased a house for them.

His purchases continued to provide for his expanding family. The compound of three large homes where I first lived was his legacy. In 1898, he became the first constable in Mount Vernon and, shortly thereafter, the first police chief. He served in that capacity for thirty-five years and retired in 1933. That's a man I'd gladly get a beer for any day.

I thought about his life frequently. My great-grandfather left all he knew to embark on his great adventure at nineteen years of age. What may have given him the reason and courage to do so? Alone in a new country, he was able to prosper, provide for his family, and serve others.

It took many years and extensive research for me to understand his influence on me. I am thankful and fortunate to have known him however slight the memory may be. I am the beneficiary of his lineage, which has given me the strength to embark on my own adventures. Just like Grandpa, I began an adventure at 19 years of age when I joined the Navy. In the future, I would follow in his footsteps to an even greater extent.

Within a year of my grandpa's death, at age 9 or 10, my mother moved us to an apartment 5 miles away from the compound. My mother was working most of the time and I no longer had the loving support of family. I began a steady downward spiral of anger, loneliness, and rebellion. The move meant a new school, and I did not easily make friends. My support system gone, I drifted aimlessly.

Even when I lived with my grandpa, I was poor. But, because I had been in a supportive and loving household, I didn't know I was poor. In our new home I was still poor but now I knew it. My mother would be at work when I got home from school. More often than not I would be hungry and unable to find anything to eat. I can remember taking a stale piece of bread and heating it up in leftover grease in the frying pan. Other times I would go to the store across the street and steal a candy bar. If I was desperate, I would walk the five miles to my grandmother's house where there was always something good to eat.

I felt embarrassed going to school because of my tattered clothing. I was growing fast, and my pants never reached my ankles. One snowy day the truant officer came to see why I wasn't in school.

"Where is your mother", he asked,

"She's at work."

"Why aren't you in school."

"It's snowing and I don't have a coat."

"Where do you keep your clothes?"

I showed him my small closet. He searched through all my clothes for a coat. When he found none, he left without saying another word. As an adult I would think back to those days. Was I really that poor or was my mother irresponsible? I think probably a combination of the two. To be fair, mom did not have it easy.

Though I struggled socially, I did make friends eventually. One of my first was Bobbie Brown. He was an easy-going, funny kid, always making jokes and laughing. We were about 12 years old when tragedy struck. Bobbie was at a county fair In Mount Vernon with two siblings and his father. His mother was at home with 4 other siblings. The house had no electricity and, at night, was lit by a kerosene lantern. Somehow, the lantern ignited the house, burning it to the ground. Bobbie's mother and 4 young siblings perished in the fire.

This tragedy instantly transformed this funny, easy-going kid into someone unrecognizable. There was no such thing as grief counseling for the class, and probably not for Bobbie. When he did return to class everyone felt uneasy in his presence. Bobbie shunned all friendships, including mine. I was so upset I remember asking my mother if Bobbie could come and live with us.

During my teenage years, I would run into Bobbie at the pool room or on the street. At times, you would see a glimpse of the old, fun-loving Bobbie, but those times were fleeting as he drifted into drug use and lack of self-esteem. When I joined the Navy, I lost track of my few childhood friends, including Bobbie. The impact of that tragedy on his life and on mine has remained with me.

There was a candy store hangout a few blocks from my house that I would frequent in hopes of being accepted by one or more kids. At fifteen I was very tall for my age. I ended up hanging out with a group of kids two to three years older than me. I was close friends with Billy and Jimmy and a couple of others. I really looked up to Billy who was always the center of attention. He had a great personality, was handsome with long blonde hair, and he had the best-looking girlfriend. At sixteen I was drinking in bars with them. I'm unsure if I was fooling anyone about my age, or if they just didn't care.

One night Billy brought me up to the pool room. It was an intimidating place, a tough place. The owner was a man, maybe 60, who ran it with an iron fist. He did not hesitate to physically throw people down the flight of stairs, which took a few minutes to walk up. He was called "Popeye," possibly after the cartoon character, but more likely because his right eye looked right at you and the left one at the ceiling. He wore glasses and always had a cigar in his mouth. Popeye booked horses and numbers openly without regard for the law. He was a scary guy, but in time, I would have the greatest respect for him.

"POPEYE"

I didn't know how to play pool and I was fearful at first, so I just sat on the side watching. Two fellows were playing 9 ball on the table closest to me, and it was obvious they were gambling. The taller of the two was a very animated attention seeker. He would win most games and collect money after each win. As he pocketed the money, he would look over toward me and grin. I was broke. I was always broke. I had no income. No allowance and no way to get any money. As I watched him pocket all that money, I remember saying to myself,

"I gotta learn how to play this game."

At 16, I went to the pool room every night and during the day, cutting school to practice. Pete was the counterman. It cost a penny a minute to play, but he gave me a lot of leeway when it wasn't busy. His prominent, thick black mustache earned him the nickname "Mustache Pete". His slicked back jet black hair tied in a short ponytail added to his distinct appearance.

Pete had twin sons a year or two younger than me. Their names were Anthony and Paul, and they were both gay. They occasionally accompanied Pete to work. He would put them to work cleaning tables or other small jobs but never allowed them to play pool. Bobbie Brown would mock their feminine movements behind Pete's back. If Pete caught Bobbie, he would throw a piece of chalk at him. Once Pete threw a cue ball at Bobbie and that stopped his taunting.

On weekends there was always a "Ring Game" where four or five players would play "Rotation" for money. Players would enter the game and lose their money, drop out, and be replaced with new money. We were only playing for nickels and dimes, but it provided me with a few dollars. These games sometimes lasted from the time the poolroom opened until it closed.

One afternoon I was in the poolroom, having cut school. There was always a lookout at the top of the stairs. He would alert Popeye to any threat from law enforcement. The illegal betting sheets would disappear in an instant. I heard the door open at the bottoms of the stairs. "Sam" the lookout called out.

"Go in the back and get under a table, quick, go."

I didn't understand this, but I quickly obeyed. Peering out from under the table I could see the same truant officer that came to my home looking around the pool room.

I dropped out of school at 16, due to my cutting classes and poor attendance. I was so far behind it just seemed impossible to catch up. I picked up a few odd jobs here and there but I'd either quit or get fired for not showing up. Instead, I was getting good at the game of pool, and I was making money. Not a lot of money but maybe like a real good allowance. If I had no money Pete would stake me, collecting forty percent of my winnings. Sometimes, Bobbie Brown would play, but he wasn't good enough to count on a steady income. I never liked playing against him because I felt bad taking his money. He wasn't a terrible player, but the drugs were taking their toll.

Popeye would periodically promote the game by having a professional pool player put on an exhibition. The pro would wow the crowd with trick shots and then play someone from the pool room. Onofrio Loria, a well-known professional player, was the pro and Popeye had me play him. We played 100 points of straight pool and I beat him badly. The poor guy did not take it very well, demonstrated by growling as he bit his cue stick. At 17, I could beat almost everybody, except for a few top players. Popeye was grooming me to play better players. But to win money he would say,

"It's not how good you play, it's who you play."

In other words, for money, you only play those you can beat.

By the time I was 19, I could beat everyone in the pool room, and I even traveled to pool rooms as far as New York City to hustle players. But there was one local exception.

Joe Black was the best player in town. I had never played him, mainly because he did not play cheap. He was a dapper guy much older than me. A sharp dresser with a lot of money in his pocket, he usually played in a poolroom across town where he was the "House Pro".

One day, coming off a win, I had about thirty dollars in my pocket. I challenged Joe to a game of 9 ball. He laughed at me and began to make a scene.

"How much you want to play for kid."

He was talking to the entire pool room as much as me.

"I'll play you for five dollars a game," I said.

That was a lot of money to me, but Joe just laughed.

"Boy, you gotta put up a lot more money than that to play Joe Black."

He continued mocking me and soon had the entire pool room on his side and laughing.

Popeye had heard enough. He stepped up to the table, reached into his pocket, and withdrew a stack of bills about two inches thick. There were twenties, fifties, hundreds. Popeye slammed the pile of money onto the pool table with a thud and then spread it across the table like a deck of cards. He first looked around at the crowd to be sure he had everyone's attention. It went dead silent; every pair of eyes was on him.

Then he looked at Joe with his good eye and said, "You play the kid for all of this, or any part of it."

The silence continued waiting for Joe Black to take up the challenge. After a feeble excuse, Joe beat a hasty retreat, leaving the pool room with laughter following him. I don't know if I could have beaten Joe Black and Popeye could not have been sure either.

Popeye, however, was good at sizing people up. He wasn't trying to make a game happen, he was defending my honor and that of his poolroom. I was the best player in his poolroom, and he was prepared to put his money on it. Whenever I was in the pool room Popeye had my back. I was young enough to be picked on by some of the bullies, but nobody dared cross Popeye.

One day I told Popeye I wanted to bet on a horse that I had received a tip on. I had never played the horses here or anywhere else. Popeye was reluctant to take my money, but eventually relented. Amazingly, the horse won, paying just a few dollars. Popeye came up to me withdrawing that huge roll of bills from his pocket, licked a finger and peeled off my winnings.

I had watched him do this many times and it always amazed me how he used the thumb on one hand to scan through the stack, efficiently stopping at the denomination he needed. First a few ones and then to the fives and tens. If he kept going, he would reveal twenties, fifties, and hundreds. Handing over my winnings Popeye pointed to a dozen customers studying racing sheets in the rear of the pool room.

"See those guys over there," he said squinting his good eye, "None of them have my money."

He pointed the good eye at me while the other seemed to be chasing a fly around the ceiling.

"I am never going to take another bet from you, and you will be the only guy in this poolroom who has my money."

"They," he said looking back at them or maybe at the ceiling, "are all losers."

Popeye was true to his word and never took another bet from me.

Playing pool for a living at age 19 had its ups and downs. I was not responsible; I didn't even know what responsibility was. I was either flush with cash or dead broke. A pool hustler is one who does whatever is necessary to take advantage of people and relieve them of their money. I didn't have what it takes to be a hustler. I didn't want to trick people out of their money, even though, at times, I did. I wanted to play the best and beat them fairly. I felt bad for people like Bobbie Brown. Compassion is fatal for a hustler.

The pool room closed at midnight. Most often, Pete, the counterman, me, and sometimes others, would go to the all-night diner a few doors down. Sometimes Bobbie Brown would join us as he knew Pete would usually pick up his tab. I enjoyed Bobbie's company during those brief periods when you could get a glimpse of the young kid. The diner was very narrow with one long counter. The short order cook was placed conveniently at the halfway point. Two waitresses split the counter in half shouting orders to the cook in the middle.

Charlie, a pool player himself, was the epitome of a short order cook. He whipped up orders for dozens of customers with nothing written down. His actions were more ballet-like, than what you might find in a midnight diner. I would watch in awe as, in one long continuous swoop he would pluck an egg from the crate, crack it, deposit it sunny side up on the griddle, and dispose of the shell. All in one motion and while tending flap jacks with the other hand.

Charlie's day off was Friday. He would stop in at the diner to pick up his pay and then come up to the poolroom to gamble with various players. Sometimes he won and sometimes he lost but he never went for much money. This Friday I was waiting for Charlie.

Pete had suggested that I try to get him into a game. Since I was broke Pete was backing me with forty percent of the winnings as his incentive. Pete was a good guy by me. I often borrowed money from him and even if I was late with repayment, he never asked for it. Pete ran numbers for Popeye. When he wasn't working at the poolroom, he was on the street picking up numbers and cash for him.

Charlie arrived on time, so I approached him immediately before he got involved elsewhere. He hesitated, as if trying to evaluate each of our games. By this time, I had a reputation as a good player. After some soul-searching Charlie declined my offer and went off looking for a better game. Pete looked at me as if to say,

"Oh well, we tried."

Several minutes later to my surprise Charlie returned.

"OK, let's go."

We started out playing 9 ball for a dollar a game. I was up about ten dollars when Charlie suggested we play for five dollars per game and shortly after ten dollars per game. Each time I looked at Pete who responded with a shrug and a nod of the head approving higher stakes. I was ahead about one hundred and twenty dollars when Charlie suggested that instead of paying after each game we pay off when one player or the other was ahead by fifty dollars. We had played two games under this new system when Pete said,

"How come he didn't pay you after the last game."

When I explained the new arrangement to Pete he said,

"No way, not on my dime! Tell him to pay up right now."

I told Charlie he had to pay after each game, and he began to cry, admitting he had no more money. He had lost his entire paycheck of one hundred and twenty dollars. He didn't have the rent and his wife would kill him. Pete was busy with customers. Charlie and I were in deep conversation. Charlie was distraught and I was feeling sorry for him, trying my best to console him. After some time, I walked back to the counter where Pete was attending to customers.

"What happened" asked Pete.

I hesitated.

"I gave him back his money."

Pete went ballistic. "You did what?"

I tried to explain to Pete that I felt sorry for the guy. Pete shrugged and gave me a bewildered look.

At that point, Charlie came over. "Let's play some more."

Now Pete and I both had a bewildered look.

I said, "Charlie, I just beat you for all your money."

He replied, "Yeah, but you gave it back to me. Let's play some more."

Pete gave me a look as if to say, this is just too incredible to be true. I was still broke and needed Pete to back me. He threw his hands up laughing.

"Sure, go ahead."

Charlie and I played again starting out at ten dollars a game. I played my best game and beat him for all his money again. This time I did it quickly and didn't give him a chance to cry on my shoulder. I gave Pete his cut and left for home with my well-deserved twice-won winnings.

I still lived in the apartment Mom, and I had moved to when I was ten. I slipped in quietly, heading for the small dinette where my fold-up bed was. I emptied the crumpled bills out of my pockets onto the bed. I was straightening out the bills and sorting them into piles of ones, fives, and tens when my mother walked in. Seeing the piles of money, she assumed I had robbed a bank or worse. The next day, she called her brother, Detective Gerald Colbert, to tell him I was a criminal and to enlist his help.

At the pool room the next evening, I had no idea that my mother had called her brother until I looked up from a shot and saw Uncle Jerry. He was big, handsome, and a well-respected Police Detective. He was also an ex-marine, although Jerry would tell you there are no ex-marines.

My heart stopped upon seeing him. Fear and embarrassment set in all at once as Uncle Jerry beckoned me. I would not think about telling him I was busy playing a game or maybe this was not a good time. I had no reason to fear him because he had always looked out for me, but this would not be good. Everyone in the poolroom had stopped what they were doing to watch this play out.

I put my cue stick down on the table and walked dutifully over to Uncle Jerry. He took me by the arm, down the stairs, and onto the sidewalk, where he calmly asked,

"What is going on? Your mother called me all upset."

Before I could say anything, Popeye came out the door.

"Jerry," he said, "can I talk to you."

That really shocked me because I had no idea, they knew each other.

Uncle Jerry told me to get in his car and wait while he spoke with Popeye. I sat nervously while they spoke for a long time. Finally, Popeye turned and went back upstairs. Jerry came over and got in the car.

"You, ok?" he asked.

"Yeah."

"OK, look, go back upstairs, do whatever Popeye tells you and don't say anything to your mother, I'll look into a couple of things, and we'll talk, ok?"

"Sure Jerry."

I could only imagine what they talked about for so long. Popeye may have said,

"Look, Jerry, while he's in my poolroom, I'll look after him. You know where he is and he's not out in the street getting into trouble."

"Yeah, something like that."

A few days later I met Uncle Jerry as requested. He said he was taking me to talk to a good friend of his. I thought I was going to counseling, or maybe prison. It turned out to be a Navy Recruiter. This was not something I would normally agree to, but, under the circumstances, I had little choice but to hear the recruiter out. It was a storefront recruiting station. Jerry introduced us and left.

The recruiter was good at his job, and he had been briefed. He knew everything about me, and I mean everything. Uncle Jerry had been tracking me long before my mother called. This wasn't just a pep talk about the Navy. It was a detailed description of how to erase the bad choices I had made. I could get my high school diploma and get training that I could use to get a real job. See the world, be a man, escape the present.

I began to realize that I was not happy with my lot in life. I was drifting aimlessly with no purpose or plan. I figured I would listen and tell him I would think about it, get back to him in a few days or so and, as always, kick the can down the road. But the punch line was yet to come. After a good hour, the recruiter hit me with it.

"Son, you have to give me your decision right now before you leave because- I have to call Jerry and let him know."

I realized the futility in trying to put this off and signed on the dotted line. Thus, I began my journey to boot camp, aviation ordnance school, and the Gulf of Tonkin with a brief stop at a marine brig.

Chapter 2

MILITARY SERVICE

Boot camp at Great Lakes Naval Training Center in December was the coldest I have ever been in my life. It was brutal, but I enjoyed the structure. My Uncle Jerry had always looked out for me, but this really changed my life for the better. It wasn't just the change that I needed; it was the different path in my life that was pivotal.

The Vietnam War broke out shortly after I deployed. Uncle Jerry confided in me years later that he had many sleepless nights, knowing he had sent me into harm's way. Every so often during my enlistment, usually when I could use it the most, I would receive a card or letter from Uncle Jerry with ten or twenty dollars enclosed. Uncle Jerry was the only person, family or not, who has never missed my birthday. Until his death, I received a card from him on every birthday of my life. My own mother couldn't say that. Many people have impacted my life, but no one more than my Uncle Jerry. Uncle

Jerry transformed my life after Grandpa George saved it.

I did well during my four years in the Navy. I got my high school diploma, finishing ahead of 97 percent of those taking the test. I graduated from Aviation Ordnance School, number one out of forty graduating students. I continued my training in Explosive Ordnance Disposal. Promotions to E4 and E5 were achieved in the shortest time possible. I participated in the historic Gulf of Tonkin incident. And yes, I made that brief and eventful stop at a Marine Brig. Not bad for a high school dropout.

Prior to boarding the USS Ticonderoga, I attended a class A school In Jacksonville, Florida, to become an AO or Aviation Ordnanceman. The classroom and practical instruction required serious attention. The hands-on work with actual explosives and munitions caught my interest. The destructive power of those objects of war gripped me with just the right amount of fear to be exhilarating.

For the first time in my life, I dedicated myself to something other than pool. Graduating at the top of my class in Aviation Ordnance School taught me a valuable life lesson: I could achieve anything I set my mind to. Several individuals dropped out of the course. Some flunked out, others failed to qualify for the Top-Secret Security clearance required for the missiles and nuclear weapons portions of the training. A sailor named Sam encountered trouble with a Marine Duty Officer.

The school was a one-story stand-alone building encircled by an 8-foot fence topped with barbed wire. Rules were explicit and rigorously enforced. All notes and books had to remain in the classroom. Inside the building were inert, but actual working models of Sidewinder missiles and nuclear weapons. Armed guards patrolled the grounds 24 hours a day. While in class, armed marines provided security. Armed students in pairs would patrol inside the fence in four-hour shifts when class was not in session.

Sam and I were on duty one evening, patrolling inside the fence. With the day ending, the area was devoid of traffic. A jeep drove up to the gate and out stepped a Marine Captain. He was wearing a black armband with the yellow letters "OD". He was the "Officer of the Day", the duty commander of the base. We spoke to him through an opening in the gate for which we had no key. He tested our knowledge of general commands, inspected our uniforms, and made comments on staying alert.

Then he turned to Sam. "Present your weapon for inspection, Sailor,"

Sam looked slightly confused but drew his weapon, ejected the magazine, and locked the slide back. He then handed it to the captain in a safe condition.

"Wow, that's pretty good," I thought.

The captain released the slide, replaced the magazine, and stuck the gun into his waistband. He got into the jeep and drove away with Sam's weapon.

"That can't be good," was my next thought.

Sam looked like he wanted to cry. After that night, I never saw Sam again. I don't know what happened to him, but I always assumed it had something to do with that damn Marine Captain.

Then there was my best friend, Karl. Each student was given a pad for taking notes with numbered pages and the word "CLASSIFIED" printed boldly at the top of each page. Even though we had been clearly told that no training materials were to leave the classroom, Karl thought it would be cool to take a page from deep within the pad and write his mother a letter. Investigators from the forerunner of NCIS, called CID, at the time, traveled to a rural town in upstate New York and intercepted the letter at his mother's home. Unbeknownst to us, an inventory of all student material was conducted every night. Karl lost his security clearance, was dropped from the program, and sent to the fleet.

Everything we studied was dangerous and that fact was drilled into us by our instructors.

"The dangerous time is not when you are new and inexperienced, but when you become comfortable with these weapons of war."

After Ordnance School and a brief trip home. I flew from San Diego, California, to Clark Air Force Base in the Philippines. From there a bus ride took me to Subic Bay Naval base to board the Aircraft Carrier USS Ticonderoga and after a few days in a transient barracks, I was told to report to the Carrier pier as the USS Ticonderoga would be pulling in that day.

Standing on the pier watching the "Mighty Ti", as it was nicknamed, pull into port was quite an experience. I was struck by the impressive size of it and by the fact it was listing twenty degrees to port. While conducting operations at sea, a destroyer escort had run into and pierced the side of Ticonderoga with its anchor. Repairs were swift, and within a week we were completing sea trials and on our way to Hong Kong.

Hong Kong was a spectacular port where I allowed my enthusiasm to get the best of me. During the day, I visited Tiger Balm Gardens and the Peak Tram Railway. That evening we were in the British Enlisted Men's Club having a few beers. Five of us from the Ticonderoga were guests of Britain's Royal Navy.

Hong Kong at the time was a British Colony, and the enlisted men's club served Britain's Royal Navy, but they also welcomed United States Navy enlisted men. Looking over the selections on the Juke Box I found a song I thought appropriate and played it too many times. The Battle of New Orleans by Johnny Horton. We found the lyrics to be very funny, particularly under the circumstances.

"We fired our guns and the British kept a'coming
There wasn't nigh as many as there was a while ago
We fired once more and they began to running on
Down the Mississippi to the Gulf of Mexico"

About the third time I played this on the Juke Box, we began to draw the attention of British Sailors. Then something happened that I don't understand to this day. A British sailor, who I might add was six feet seven inches tall, went to the Juke Box and pulled the plug when the Battle of New Orleans played for the umpteenth time. He went back to his table, climbed on top of it, rolled up a newspaper so it was like three feet long, pulled down his pants, put the newspaper between his legs, and lit both ends on fire. He began to dance about on top of the table with fire threatening his buttocks and scrotum.

This display was interrupted when a beer mug crashed onto our table thrown by one of our hosts. There were probably one hundred people in the club, of which twenty to thirty were US sailors. Now bottles, mugs, and fists were flying.

The fight spilled out into an alley. I was confronted by Mr. Six Foot Seven, who was hell-bent on my destruction. At six foot four, I was no slouch, but our fight was preempted by Shore Patrol from both countries. I offered no resistance to the United States Marine Sergeant who grabbed and handcuffed me. Nonetheless, he pushed me into the Paddy wagon with such force that I missed the two steps getting into it and opened a large gash on my shin. I also struck my head on the door frame creating a good-sized laceration and lump.

On the way back to the ship I managed to get out of the handcuffs. When the Marine Sergeant opened the door, I chinned myself on the door frame and came out feet first, planting both feet in the middle of his chest, knocking him down and landing on top of him. Since the sergeant was not alone, I lost that fight.

I had to be treated in Sick Bay for my injuries which, fortunately for me, were well-documented. To my knowledge, the sergeant sustained no visible damage. My Summary Court Martial came quickly, as did the guilty verdict with a sentence of 30 days in the Brig.

This was a career-ending event. I was scheduled to be transferred from the Ticonderoga to a land-based brig. After that, it was anyone's guess what might happen to me. I was temporarily placed in the ship's brig pending transfer. Every prisoner had the right to draft a letter to Captain Clark, the ship's Commanding Officer upon entering the ship's brig. I had no expectation that the captain would get the letter and even less that he would read or act on it. Still, I drafted a three-page letter pouring my heart out while taking full responsibility for my actions.

On the second night I was incarcerated aboard ship the Catholic Chaplain came to see me. We spoke about the incident, and my remorse for being involved. The Chaplain began telling me what a nice person the Marine Sergeant was and that he had a family that depended on him. He then asked me to recant my statement indicating the abusive treatment I had received at the hands of the sergeant. He further stated that if I recanted my testimony, which obviously caused the sergeant some jeopardy, he might put in a good word for me. It was then I realized the Chaplain was not visiting on my behalf but on behalf of the sergeant.

"Are you asking me to be untruthful, Father?"

The conversation ended abruptly with the chaplain obviously displeased with the results of his proposal.

I fully expected to be transferred from the ship to the base brig but that did not happen. On my fifth day in the ship's brig, I was advised that I was being transferred, but not to another brig. Instead, I found myself transferred back to my division as if nothing had happened. Captain Clark had intervened by squashing the Court Martial and passing a sentence of five days in the brig for my part in the incident. I wrote the captain another letter thanking him for his actions and telling him I would make him proud. One safety enhancement that came out of this was the British Enlisted Men's Club forever after served all drinks in paper cups. I would think taking Johnnie Horton and the Battle of New Orleans off the Juke Box would also be prudent.

The flight deck of an aircraft carrier is choreographed chaos, with noise levels off the chart, jet blasts that can send bodies flying, and jet intakes that have the power to suck you off your feet and chew you up. Propellers spin just fast enough to be both invisible and deadly. Add to that the presence of bombs, rockets, napalm, and other deadly weapons of war. Those dangers were in simultaneous motion, make a mistake, and there would not be a second chance.

Flight deck crew members wore shirts of various colors that designated job responsibilities. Catapult and arresting gear crew had green shirts, brown shirts for the aircraft deck crew, white were medical corpsmen, and so on. My shirt was red, signifying ordnance. Yellow shirts were officers and supervisors who coordinated various functions into one seamless operation. The job always got done, but sometimes danger could not be avoided.

My job on the flight deck consisted of two primary responsibilities. The first was to form 20mm canon shells into long continuous belts and the second was to prepare napalm bombs. The 20mm belts were formed by a six-man crew in the belting shack just under the flight deck. Three men fed cannon shells each with a different explosive charge and a fourth man fed the links into a machine. A few hours work would result in dozens of one hundred and twenty-five round belts for the F8 Crusaders main weapon.

My second function was to prepare dreaded napalm bombs. I say dreaded because everybody feared them. They were dangerous to prepare to say nothing of the fumes one must endure during the process. They were a horrific weapon of war, putting fear into the enemy. Aircraft were not permitted to land on the carrier should a napalm bomb get hung up. If a land base was not available, the pilot had no choice but to bail out into the ocean and hope he would be picked up.

The prime weapon of the F8 Crusaders was its 20mm canon, although it also carried Zuni rockets and Sidewinder missiles. It was intimidating on the flight deck and in the air. The F8 Crusader had a top speed of 1000 mph. When landing on the flight deck, the ship would increase speed to mitigate its steep landing force.

The A4 Skyhawk had 5 weapons stations to mount ordnance. It could carry bombs and rockets plus a two-thousand-pound napalm bomb on its center station.

Prior to August 1964 the United States had denied any direct military involvement in Vietnam. As history will tell us, however, we had been deeply involved for some time.

The following events chronicle how a few thousand close friends, and I started the Vietnam War.

The USS Ticonderoga was backup for the USS Maddox. We had been on alert for days, fearing hostilities by Vietnamese Torpedo Fast Boats. Maddox was patrolling close to the shore and around North Vietnamese held islands, intercepting radio transmissions and passing information to a secret CIA operation. South Vietnam forces used the intelligence gathered by the naval ships to exploit weaknesses and conduct attacks and shelling of coastal targets in the North.

On August 2, 1964, North Vietnam People's Navy torpedo boats confronted the destroyer, USS Maddox. The Maddox fired warning shots at the approaching boats and the North Vietnamese attacked with torpedoes and machine gun fire. In defense, Maddox retaliated with its five-inch deck guns.

Anticipating the attack, two F8 Crusaders were at the ready, one on each catapult. Pilots were on board with jet engines ignited and ready to go. Two more F8s were ready to move up. The distress call came in, Maddox was under attack. Within seconds, Ticonderoga had launched two F8 Crusaders with their deadly cargo. The jets were over the target within minutes, engaging and destroying three fast boats with 20mm cannon fire. Maddox destroyed another fast boat with its deck gun. The Maddox evaded at least three torpedoes and survived a few bullet holes from machine gun fire.

The next morning, USS Turner Joy, joined Maddox. Both ships pulled alongside Ticonderoga one at a time to top off their fuel, which we delivered by highline. A severely injured crewman from the previous day's engagement was high lined to the Ticonderoga for treatment.

High-line transfers were an essential element of US Navy combat operations. Two ships sail in close parallel, maintaining a precise distance apart. The process begins with shooting a line from one ship to the other. The initial line was lightweight and used to pull across heavier ropes or cables that would serve as the high line. Once the high line was securely established, the transfer commenced, including hoses for fuel and cables for solid goods and munitions.

After refueling, Ticonderoga, Maddox, and Turner Joy steamed full speed ahead, three abreast for some time. The scene was incredibly awe-inspiring. It demonstrated solidarity for the task that lay ahead. One by one, the destroyers peeled off.

August 4th brought another attack on Maddox and Turner Joy. This time Turner Joy put in the distress call for help. Ticonderoga again launched Jets to repel the attack. Pilots reported engaging the enemy, but conditions were such that contacts were brief and inconclusive. The height of the waves had increased, and visibility was low.

After the second attack on Maddox and Turner Joy, the Ticonderoga task force received orders from the President of the United States.

"Destroy the torpedo boat base and infrastructure at Haiphong Harbor from where the attack emanated."

The mission was scheduled for August 5th, a day that changed the course of history and profoundly impacted me. Years from that date I would suffer from PTSD and survivor's guilt. I would find myself drawn to the Vietnam Memorial in Washington, DC, seeking closure. The repeated haunting dreams seemed to have no end.

There would be little to no sleep for 36 hours. Bombs, rocket motors, warheads, and fuses were gathered deep within the ship. Assembly areas were set up for bombs, rockets, sidewinder missiles, and 20mm ammunition belts. The F8 Crusaders would also provide "Carrier Air Protection" armed with Sidewinder air-to-air missiles. Assembled munitions were placed on skids ready for delivery to the squadrons for loading on aircraft by skilled crewmen.

On the morning of August 5th, 1964, the ship's crew did not hear the normal wake-up announcement. Instead, there was a loud klaxon followed by,

"This is not a drill", "This is not a drill," "General Quarters, General Quarters, all hands man your Battle Stations." We were about to declare war on North Vietnam with a devastating air attack.

At dawn on August 5th, I had a dozen bomb skids tied down and loaded with 250-pound bombs on the outboard side of the island structure. More were standing by at the hangar bay assembly point. As soon as the launch was complete, we would run those skids out to the squadrons for loading on aircraft.

I would deliver dozens of bombs to Aviation Ordnanceman Joe Williams, who was in charge of all ordnance for his squadron. Joe Williams was a career professional first-class Petty Officer. He was friendly and willing to pitch in to help his crew with the heavy work or anyone needing a hand. I would see Joe that morning, but not the way I expected.

As I lowered the deck plate for the number two bomb elevator, I heard a screeching sound behind the island structure. There was a commotion some fifty feet away, just out of sight. My first thought, as I sprinted toward the sound, was that one or more of my bomb skids, each with 750 pounds of ordnance, had broken loose.

As I rounded the corner at the end of the island structure, a horrific sight confronted me. My first glance went to the bomb skids which I could see were secure. Simultaneously taking in the entire scene, I observed the radar plane, an E1B "Tracer" two-engine propeller aircraft, parked in the first spot behind the Island. This was unusual since this spot was normally reserved for our AD3 Sky Warrior Nuclear Bomber. Over the past three years, I had never seen the Radar Plane in this spot. The propeller blades were just coming to a stop. The side of the craft was covered with blood as if paint had been flicked from a paintbrush. Beneath the wing was the form of a man. Despite the blood and twisted body, I could see that his shirt was red, just like mine. I could not immediately identify him, but I knew he was one of us, an Aviation Ordnanceman.

I would later find out it was Joe Williams. He was a person I respected and worked with every day.

Joe had come up to the flight deck from the hanger deck via a catwalk behind the aircraft, a route I often took. It was a shortcut not known by many. The only plane ever parked in this spot was the A3D bomber, a jet aircraft not capable of causing the carnage in front of me.

The E1-b Tracer was a 2-engine Carrier Early Warning radar plane nicknamed "Willie Fudd." A large radar dome on top of the fuselage was a distinguishing feature. It was to be launched next to provide Ticonderoga early warning of any approaching aircraft. When Joe arrived on the Flight deck, the radar plane was still tied down and the crew had just fired up the engines. The spinning blades would be virtually invisible. The deafening noise on the flight deck would make identifying any individual engine noise unlikely.

The plane captain was on deck communicating with the pilot by hand signals. As I approached the area, I saw him move his hand across his throat signaling the pilot to cut the engines. The blades did not stop in time to save Joe, but there was no blame to be assigned. The flight deck is a dangerous place. Crewmembers need to be aware of the dangers as they go about their business.

Joe confidently came on deck as he did every day expecting to walk securely under the wing of the A3D Bomber but instead into the deadly arc of those blades. His death was tragic for him and his family. His death would be a burden I would carry for a lifetime. Combat air operations stalled briefly while Joe was tended to and removed on a stretcher. They washed the blood down with a fire hose and the war continued.

The air attack was a great success. Pilots reported huge columns of smoke rising from the oil depot. The Zuni rockets performed as expected, penetrating the oil storage tanks and detonating deep inside, causing huge explosions. Over twenty-five torpedo fast boats were destroyed. All pilots returned safely. The Gulf of Tonkin incident was in the history books, and we were at war.

We stayed on station for an extended period conducting bombing runs daily. Every couple of days a replenishment ship would pull alongside. We would get food by highline, Fuel, and even 250-pound bombs. Transferring these munitions at sea was scary and dangerous. An explosion was not likely but four 250-pound bombs swinging wildly in a net as it is brought aboard was a serious threat.

The one overwhelming danger always on my mind to the point of obsession was going over the side and into the ocean. Tragically, crewmen have been lost this way in the recent past and others will be lost in the future.

I came close to going over the side, possibly never to be seen again. The chilling event would revisit me as recurring nightmares and post-traumatic stress for many years. I was supervising munitions being assembled for a strike in support of South Vietnamese forces. Gary, an ordnance crewmen yelled out that he had a problem.

"Fred, there's something wrong with this fuse."

"It's not screwed in all the way," I replied after a casual glance.

"It won't go in any further," Gary said.

I took a closer look and then tried turning the fuse. It wouldn't budge in either direction.

"Did you cross-thread it?" I asked.

"No, it just stopped going in".

Fusing bombs is routine, and any ordnance crewman can do it. Removing the fuse is a different matter calling for EOD or "Explosive Ordnance Disposal" expertise. We would use several types of fuses, including an anti-withdrawal fuse. On any given mission, we prepared some bombs with anti-withdrawal fuse types. In that case, the released bomb would drop to the target without exploding. The enemy would remove the fuse to use the explosive for their own purpose, but if they were to unscrew an anti-withdrawal fuse, the bomb would detonate. I examined the fuse carefully and decided it was a normal impact fuse. However, I still hesitated to forcefully remove it.

"Jesus, Gary, what the fuck did you do?"

Gary Buckwell was one of the first friends I made aboard ship. He was quiet and withdrawn. A third-class petty officer, he had failed promotional tests three times. Gary was picked on by his fellow shipmates due to his withdrawn, sometimes incompetent nature. I don't like bullies and had a soft spot for their victims, so I befriended Gary to shield him from abuse. Gary taught me how to play chess as a reward. He could sure screw up most things like fusing a bomb but as a chess player and teacher he was a genius.

Gary said, "Maybe we should call the Chief."

"No time," I replied. "I'm gonna get rid of this thing over the side."

Master Chief Waste oversaw anything and everything that explodes. He was our go-to Explosive Ordnance

Disposal tech. He would rarely come to the flight deck, even though it was his duty station. He trained me to deal with most anything that would require his attention. I did my job by doing his.

The bomb was on a two-wheel bomb skid. The skid had a long handle which acted as a counterweight.

"Gary, take all the tie-downs off, I'll run it off the back of the flight deck."

"That's crazy, man."

"Just do it," I said. "We can't load this on a plane, and we can't put it back in the magazine with a fucking fuse in it."

The end of the flight deck was a short distance away. I strained to move the skid for the first few feet until the weight of the bomb and inertia took over. As I neared the edge of the flight deck, I was at a trot, trying to keep up with the skid. At the last moment, I stopped and leaned back, holding onto the skid handle, expecting the bomb to slide off the skid and into the ocean far below. The bomb and the skid remained inseparable, and the three of us were going over the side.

"I can't hold it." I blurted out in panic.

Letting go at the last moment to save myself, the bomb and skid went off the deck and into the ocean. Standing on one foot at the edge of the flight deck with a delicate balance weighted toward the ocean side, I looked down at the ship's wake churning 60 feet below.

Even if I survived the fall, I would most certainly drown. Abruptly, my balance shifted, my arms swimming in midair, desperately trying to find something to grab on to. Battling gravity with all my might, I threw myself back onto the deck.

Gary ran over, "Man, you almost bought it."

Yeah, I almost bought it for sure. There was a moment where I accepted my fate as I balanced precariously looking down at the ocean. Something pulled me back onto the deck. Whether it was sheer will to live or an unknown power I can only wonder.

My discharge date drew near. The next time we pulled into Subic Bay, Philippines, I would be leaving Ticonderoga. The ship's executive officer called me in for a talk and offered me an alternative to going home.

If I were to reenlist on the spot, I could name my next duty station. I would be guaranteed a Class A school and promotion to Chief Petty Officer soon after. He reached into a drawer and removed a roll of one-hundred-dollar bills, which he began counting until he had an impressive stack sitting in front of me. He pointed to the money.

"Sign up right now, and you can take the money with you."

Aviation Ordnanceman was a critical specialty. Now, with a new war, it was more critical than ever. It takes time to put an AO through school and the dropout rate is high due to the complex nature of the material and required security clearance. Onboard an aircraft carrier every bomb, bullet, and missile delivered to the enemy passes through the hands of an Aviation Ordnanceman.

I told the XO I would think about it, but I knew I wanted to go home. I did not give consideration to the fact that my success in the Military might not reflect how I would do as a civilian. Certainly, the last time I was a civilian, things were messy. The Navy had done more for me than I could ever imagine. My transformation from an unstable nineteen-year-old kid to someone the United States government trusted with nuclear weapons was testimony to that.

Ticonderoga pulled into our base at Subic Bay, Philippines, in early November 1964. I received my orders and disembarked Ticonderoga for the last time. I had made a few close friends on the "TI," but for some reason, I avoided saying my goodbyes and left the ship unceremoniously. On the Pier, a bus was waiting to take me to Clark Air Force Base, where I would catch a flight to San Diego, California.

Upon Arrival at Clark Airforce Base, I was assigned a bunk in a transient barracks. I could not believe how Air Force enlisted men lived. I had a single bunk, not three stacked high as on the ship. A spacious closet accommodated clothing on hangers, ample drawer and shelf space was available. The Airforce even provided an ironing board with an iron. After settling in, I searched for and found the Airforce Enlisted Men's Club. I again found splendor not known to any seagoing Naval enlisted man. This turned out to be my hangout for more evenings than I had anticipated.

I was instructed to stay packed and check in with the personnel department each morning to determine if I had a flight scheduled. Weeks went by with no luck. A couple of times, I was told "tomorrow," only to have it canceled at the last minute. It was evident that many people were heading back to the States. They prioritized wounded personnel, officers, and, I guess, those with clout.

One night, I was in the Enlisted Men's Club and happened to meet up with a guy I knew from the personnel office. Complaining to him about my situation, he unexpectedly said,

"Hey, I can get you out of here tomorrow."

"Wow, great, I'm already packed."

However, there was one major drawback. I would be a "Prison Chaser". I knew the term meant escorting a prisoner from one location to another. It was a way home, so I agreed.

I reported to Personnel the next morning as instructed. I received my orders and was told to pick up my prisoner at the Marine Brig, a concept I was familiar with. God bless the Marines, but I hate them. They are so formal and kind of stuffy. They are always fighting a war, even if there isn't one.

I felt very uncomfortable walking into the Brig in my Dress whites. There has always been this rivalry between the Navy and the Marines. They dress better but are not as smart. I was escorted into the office of the Marine Commandant for instructions. The whole left side of his shirt was covered with ribbons. He didn't speak; he barked instead. I began thinking I was going to be the prisoner.

I received a briefing on my charge. He was on his way to Federal Prison after Courts Martial found him guilty of Attempted Murder of a Chief Petty Officer. He had stabbed the chief several times after an undisclosed argument. I should consider him dangerous and an escape risk.

They assigned a third-Class Petty Officer to assist me with his transport. I was issued a standard 45 caliber pistol with belt and holster and a pair of handcuffs, all of which I had to sign for with the threat of my own imprisonment if they were lost or stolen. My assistant was issued a wooden Billy Club with a belt and scabbard. His third-class rank was subordinate to my second-class rank and of course, my 45 pistol trumped his wooden club.

The Marine Commandant gave me very specific instructions regarding the sidearm. It was to be carried with a full magazine inserted and an empty chamber. I was not to give possession of this pistol to anyone, including my assistant. The only person I would turn this pistol over to would be the Marine Commandant in the San Diego Brig. A Marine escort would meet us at the airport in San Diego.

"Understood."

"Yes, sir."

"One last thing, if he escapes you serve his time."

I didn't think that was true, but I wasn't going to take any chances.

We went inside the brig to get the prisoner, who the Marines strip-searched in my presence. He was young, about 20 years old, of average size but clearly scared to death. The Marines barked commands at him as marines are known to do. They were borderline abusive to him which I wanted to object to but used discretion. Once handed over to me, I would take control and establish the parameters. It was my first experience with a prisoner, but it would be far from my last.

We were to take a commercial flight from a nearby airport. A marine escort drove us to the airport about an hour from Clark Airforce Base. Once in the terminal and shed of the Marine escort, I had a talk with my prisoner. If he did what he was told I would treat him fairly.

"We have a long trip ahead of us and I will do my best not to embarrass or bring undue attention to you."

This talk was just as much for the Petty Officer assisting me as it was for the prisoner. The prisoner seemed very relieved and agreeable. He offered no problems all the way back and, in the end, I felt very sorry for him.

We were informed that our flight was ready, and arrangements had been made for us to be the first to board. We proceeded to the tarmac. A stewardess standing at the bottom of the stairs greeted us. Noticing that I was armed, she informed me that I could not board with a weapon. I advised her that there was no option, I would board with the weapon because I was on official military business.

"Wait here." She ascended the stairs to get the captain.

The pilot came down the stairs and analyzed the problem. He repeated the same prohibition.

"You cannot come aboard a commercial airliner carrying a sidearm". Again, I insisted, citing US Military Official Business.

He looked at me sympathetically and said, "OK, I'll tell you what. Give me the sidearm, and I'll keep it in the cockpit until we get to San Diego."

I recalled vividly the Marine Commandant's admonition that I should not allow anyone to take possession of the weapon.

"Sir, I cannot do that," I stated firmly.

The captain looked me squarely in the eye and said, "Son, you're not flying today."

Without further hesitation, I unhooked my belt, wrapped it around the holstered pistol, and handed it to the captain. Damn the consequences,

"I am flying today."

The captain had one more instruction, to which I agreed without argument. I could board the aircraft with the prisoner handcuffed and seat him. However, I must remove the handcuffs before takeoff and for the duration of the flight.

It was a long flight, but it proceeded without incident. According to plan, a Marine escort met us at the gate. Without so much as "How was your flight?", they began to humiliate my prisoner in front of countless civilians at the airport.

The corporal tried to aggressively place him against a wall to search him in the busy terminal as passengers gawked.

My determination to have them back off almost became physical. They finally backed off when I stated firmly:

"You are interfering with my prisoner."

I had retrieved my sidearm from the pilot and placed my hand on it as a sign I was dead serious. We proceeded without further incident, and, to my surprise, there was no mention of this confrontation upon arrival at the brig.

I really felt bad for the kid. I thanked him for his cooperation and wished him luck. He disappeared into the depths of the brig. My assistant went his separate way and I needed to turn in my sidearm. It was late in the day.

The senior Marine at the brig was a duty officer. When I attempted to give him my sidearm, he refused to accept it.

"You need to turn that in at Personnel."

It didn't sound right, but I was tired and didn't want to argue with another Marine.

It was even later when I arrived at personnel and encountered a "Navy Duty Officer".

"I can't take your sidearm, but I'll assign you a bunk in the transient barracks and you can figure it out in the morning."

When I arrived at the transient barracks, it was midnight, and I was dog tired. I put the pistol under my pillow and went to sleep.

It was still dark when I was violently shaken awake, a flashlight beam disorienting me. Someone was yelling the same phrase over and over. It wasn't until I heard it for the third time that I began to make sense of what was going on.

"Where's the fucking gun!?"

Someone finally turned on a light and it took a few more seconds for me to adjust.

'Damn, more Marines.'

This time, it was a Marine Captain wearing the "Duty Officer" armband and his driver. He repeated the phrase again. When I showed him, it was under my pillow, he became enraged, yelling at me as Marines tend to. My explanation did not improve his attitude. I was about to ask him for a receipt when he took possession of the gun, turned, and stormed out. No sense pushing my luck.

San Diego was a major mustering-out location. Before my official discharge, I was scheduled for a comprehensive physical exam. All was good except for the hearing test. Years on the flight deck had taken their toll. It was the morning of my discharge date, and the doctor was giving me the results.

"Everything is great except your hearing, most notably in your left ear." He said, "If you hang around for a couple of days, we can probably get you a disability rating."

"No thanks, I'm outta here."

Yeah, big mistake on my part. It would be years before I would finally petition the VA for disability ratings related to my hearing deficit, Agent Orange exposure, and Post Traumatic Stress Disorder.

As a parting gift, I received my Honorable Discharge, DD214, which is a record of my service, medical history, and a list of civilian occupations to which my training qualified me. I was going home, hopefully as a smarter, more responsible civilian than when I enlisted.

Aviation Ordnance Crew
Author standing left, circa 1964

Chapter 3

THERE'S A NEW SHERIFF
IN TOWN

Once I arrived back in San Diego, processing only took a few days. I received my discharge papers and looked for a way home. I met two Navy guys who were driving to Philadelphia and wanted someone to share expenses. It worked out great for me. I took a train into New York City from Philadelphia, then a taxi from Grand Central Terminal to Mount Vernon.

The taxi drove up the avenue past the all-night diner and the poolroom. Out on the sidewalk and spilling into the street were pool tables in various stages of destruction. Two men wielding sledgehammers were breaking the pool table slates into smaller pieces.

"I'll have to find a real job," I thought.

I wanted to do something meaningful after my military experience. In the Navy, I had responsibility, and I was recognized for my abilities with promotions and an honorable discharge. I shuddered to think how I had put that in jeopardy by my actions in Hong Kong. I had no intentions of going backward but had no idea what to do going forward. To better myself, I'd need to find a good job and stay out of pool rooms.

The dreams started shortly after I got home. At the time, I had no idea what PTSD, or Post Traumatic Stress Disorder, was, but looking back, I had a severe case of it. Over the years, it got better but never went away completely. One dream I had repeatedly was of me treading water in the middle of the ocean, the Ticonderoga sailing off in the distance.

Back on the "Ti" I would sleep on a catwalk just off the flight deck. It was, in fact, the catwalk that Joe Williams used on the day he died. That catwalk was simply a grill that connected the flight deck to the deck directly below. It was 3 feet wide and 15 feet long, with a simple handrail for safety. The mist from the ocean below coming up through the grill had a cooling effect. It was remote and not a normal travel route, making it ideal for my purpose.

I had never thought about it at the time, but if I'd rolled over, I would have fallen off the catwalk and into the ocean far below. That's exactly what would happen in my dream. It was terrifying, but I would never hit the water because I would awake with a start, terrified and sweating profusely.

In the worst dream, Joe Williams was torn apart by propeller blades in a gruesome death. That dream had a lot of versions to it. One had me walking into the propeller blades. In another version I was unsuccessfully trying to save Joe. In some of my dreams, I watch Joe walk into the spinning propeller, but I am frozen, and I can't move. The dreams occurred as I slept, but they would also creep into my daytime activities.

I took the same route to the flight deck as Joe Williams. Could I have made the same fatal mistake that Joe did? One of my responsibilities was the 20 mm belting shack, where cannon ammunition was stored and formed into continuous belts. That magazine was directly below where Joe was killed. It was the quickest route from the belting shack to the flight deck. Yes, it could have been me.

Five years after my discharge date, the dreams were terrible. I was watching a documentary on television about Vietnam veterans and the challenges that made some drop out of society. The interviewer was speaking to a disheveled man who lived off the grid in Hawaii. He grew marijuana and spoke of the horrors he experienced as a grunt in Vietnam. The man had obvious mental issues that were laid bare as he related his experiences. The next two veterans were similar in that they had dropped out of society and were experiencing PTSD and other mental issues. As I watched, I felt a kinship with those men.

Then there was the man in upstate New York who lived in a homemade shelter and fished in a nearby stream for his only food source. He related his story while sobbing. He said he was on the flight deck of an aircraft carrier when he saw a man walk into a spinning propeller blade. He was close enough to grab the man but froze and failed to do so. He was overwhelmed with guilt and remorse over the man's death on the USS Ticonderoga.

I was stunned that he and I had witnessed the death of Joe Williams so many years ago. I didn't know him and did not know of anyone who witnessed what I did on that day. He must have been standing within arm's reach of me. We shared a traumatic event. Did we also share the resulting mental illness?

I tried to evaluate myself to determine how far gone I was, but I couldn't be objective. I knew I had periodic anger issues and of course, dreams terrified me and disturbed my sleep. Simple things easily irritated me, which frequently led to punching a wall or breaking something out of frustration.

I decided to contact some of my old friends from the Ticonderoga to see if they were screwed up too. The first one I tried to contact was Jack. We were pretty close, and if anyone was screwed up, it would be him. I remembered that he lived in a small upstate New York town, making it easy to track him down.

When I left the Ticonderoga, I never said goodbye to my friends and never tried to contact them afterward. It made me feel guilty and ashamed because we were so close. In San Diego, our home port, we had membership in a locker club storing civilian clothes and other personal items. We would come ashore in uniform and then go to the locker club to change into civilian clothes. I thought maybe if I played a little joke on Jack, it would help break the ice.

When Jack answered the phone,

I said, "Is Mr. Tinkler at home?"

He answered, "This is Mr. Tinkler."

"Hello, Mr. Tinkler; this is Homer Smith from the Seven Seas Locker Club in San Diego, California."

I paused to let that sink in, realizing it would invoke a WTF moment.

I continued, "Mr. Tinkler, we have just opened a locker that was long forgotten, and it seems it belonged to you."

His reply sounded like, "Uh huh."

I continued trying to sound serious. "This locker contained some clothing, photographs, and personal papers, and I was wondering if you would like me to send them to you?"

Jack replied, "Well yes, that would be great."

I said, "Fine, Mr. Tinkler, we'll get the contents in the mail to you right away, there is just one minor detail."

He replied, "What is that?"

I said, "It's a matter of five years of past due locker rent. It comes to two thousand, four hundred and twenty-five dollars and eighteen cents."

There was a very long pause.

His reply. "Kenney, is that you?"

"Yeah Jack, how ya doin?"

Separated by five years, we picked up right where we left off. We spoke of other friends Jack was in touch with and the fact that the Veterans Administration was sending him beer money because of a service-related injury.

Then he asked, "Hey, do you ever hear from Sergeant Brown?"

I laughed; Sergeant Brown was the Marine that got me thrown into the brig.

Jack said, "Yeah, he don't want nothing to do with those size twelves you put in the middle of his chest."

We both had a good laugh. On the same day that Joe Williams was killed, Jack had his hand crushed when a two-hundred-and-fifty-pound bomb failed to lock in on the bomb rack and fell back onto the skid, pinning his hand. He had surgery aboard ship, putting the bones back in place. He regained use of his hand, even though all the fingers pointed in the wrong direction.

Jack seemed to be the same as I had always known him, and I didn't mention the dreams I was having. It was nice reconnecting, and we concluded our conversation with pledges to visit one day.

Fresh out of the Navy, I needed to find a job. Some suggested that I look for a job in civil aviation at a commercial airport. The idea was to apply to an airline or airport and figure out what might be available to someone with my expertise.

I had considered following in the footsteps of family members like Uncle Jerry or Grandpa George and becoming a police officer. Upon investigation, I found that all forty-four police agencies in Westchester County drafted recruits from a common list that came from a test given every two years or more. That test had just been given, and only those on the list had a chance of being hired.

I succeeded in scheduling an interview with an airline at the nearby airport. The airline manager's office was in a hangar at the far side of the airport. A receptionist ushered me into his office.

After being invited to have a seat, he asked, "What is it you can do for this airline?"

His appearance and gruff demeanor surprised me. He wore a fedora and smoked a cigar. Sitting behind his desk, I could tell he was short and pudgy. This was not the appearance I had expected of an airline manager.

"Well sir, I am not sure what positions you have open, but I have been working in and around aircraft for the past four years."

"Ok," he said, "tell me more."

Upon this invitation, I opened up about working on the flight deck of an aircraft carrier, with the responsibility for all ordnance coming to the flight deck. I mentioned Aviation Ordnance school, my promotions to AO3 and AO2, and my supervisory responsibilities. He looked interested, maybe even impressed, and I thought I was doing pretty good. I withheld any mention of nuclear weapons, even though I felt it may impress him. I wouldn't want him to think I would give up military secrets. When I finished, there was silence for a few moments. Then he broke it,

"Son, American Airlines does not hang bombs on the wings of our airplanes."

He paused to let that sink in. Then he continued.

"Rockets would make the passengers very nervous."

I could see where this was going.

"And if we were to open the bomb bay doors, all of the luggage would fall out."

He was enjoying this.

"Why don't you find a company that needs the decks swabbed or something painted."

So much for my military training and transition to a civilian job. Humiliated and embarrassed, I thanked him for his time and hurriedly left, totally disheartened.

All seemed hopeless until George Martin, the next person to alter the trajectory of my life, unexpectedly stepped in. I was invited to a fundraiser for the Republican Party. It was an open invitation to anyone who would put up twenty-five dollars for a prime rib dinner. I had no intention of getting involved in politics and was not even a registered Republican. I'm not sure why I went, other than it was something to do.

Sitting at a table with a group of men, it became apparent I was the stranger in the group. By way of introduction, I let it be known that I recently had been discharged from the military. There were a lot of questions and interest shown in my experiences.

This was a patriotic group and they expressed approval and thanked me for my service. A frail older gentleman among them was particularly interested in me personally. That was George Martin, and he wanted to know more about my desire to be a police officer.

I told him about my family's history with law enforcement and my ambition to follow in their footsteps. When I mentioned my grandfather, he let me know he was well acquainted with the name. He understood my dilemma with the next test being at least two years away.

George asked me if I was familiar with the Sheriff's Department. I joked that the only sheriff I was familiar with was in cowboy movies. Little did I know that soon I would be confronted with modern-day Sheriffs and cowboys.

George explained that the Sheriff was the most powerful Lawman in the County because he was the only one elected by the public. Deputy Sheriff's don't come off a list. They are appointed by the Sheriff. This was already beginning to sound promising when George came right to the point.

"I have a good friend in the Sheriff's Department, how about I take you up there to meet him tomorrow."

"That sounds great."

George insisted we take his car since there would be no place for me to park. George was frail, barely able to peer over the dashboard of his well-kept but old car. We pulled into the parking lot of the County Court House, where every parking space had a designated sign for a judge, District Attorney, or Law enforcement officer but none for visitors. George pulled into a space reserved for "Sheriff's Department". I was about to express concern when George produced a sign and placed it on his dashboard. "Official Business, Sheriff's Department"

George was well-known and was greeted by people as we entered the courthouse. We stopped in front of a door marked "Warrant Squad." George opened the door and ushered me in first. This made me uncomfortably conspicuous when several people in the office stopped what they were doing to peer at me. Then George came out from behind me.

"Hey George, how are you doing?" said one, taking the pressure off me.

"Billy is in the back, I'll get him."

Billy McNeil was head of the Sheriff's Warrant Squad. A grey-haired, red-faced man with a huge girth greeted George with what I discerned as deep respect. Billy listened intently as I related my military experience and desire to become a police officer. He had one question for me.

"Are you a registered Republican?"

"No sir," I replied.

"Ok," he said. "Go across the street to voter registration and register as a Republican. Then come back here first thing in the morning."

The next morning, Billy took me to the personnel department to fill out an application. I spent most of the morning filling out papers and getting my fingerprints and photograph taken. Billy and I went to lunch and had a chance to get fully acquainted. I was amazed to find out that our family history was in sync. Billy knew my Uncle Jerry, which was not so surprising, but also that our grandfathers and great-grandfathers were all in law enforcement and had close ties to each other. He knew all about my Grandpa George Atwell, who, according to Billy, was close to his family's early history in Mount Vernon.

After lunch, Billy said, "Next, we meet the sheriff. Once he approves, you'll be sworn in as a Deputy Sheriff."

I couldn't believe how quickly this was all unfolding. Just a few days ago I'd never even heard of George Martin or Billy McNeil. I had no viable path to becoming a police officer. I began to wonder about those who had impacted and changed the course of my life. Grandpa Atwell, Uncle Jerry, Popeye, Pete, Captain Clark and now George Martin and Billy McNeil. I had to do my part, but they had each helped me chart the direction.

When we arrived at the sheriff's office, he was not in. Billy told the sheriff's secretary, Mazie, why I was there and that I was to wait for the sheriff's return.

"I've got to get back," said Billy, "check with me when you're finished here."

An hour or so later, the sheriff arrived, went straight into his office, and closed the door. He was older and smaller than I had imagined. The secretary went into his office and, upon returning, smiled at me as she made a brief phone call. I took this as a sign that the sheriff was aware of my presence and when Billy walked in, I realized he was the subject of the call.

"The sheriff is ready for you Billy," said Mazie.

Billy entered the office first, with me right behind him.

"Is this your boy?" said the sheriff.

"Yes, he is, Sheriff."

The Sheriff then looked at me with squinted eyes. "You a registered Republican, boy?"

"Yes, I am, sir," I said, remembering my recent trip to voter registration. I would later find out that the Sheriff's staff referred to him fondly as "the squinty eyed bastard."

"Do you want him in the Warrant Squad, Billy?"

"Yes sir, I have an opening," Billy replied.

"Yes," said the sheriff, "a very unfortunate one."

That opening was created two weeks prior with the service of an eviction notice. Two deputies were tasked, but one decided to wait in the car while the other deputy served the notice, breaking protocol. Upon hearing gunfire, the deputy in the car sped off to the local police department for help. The Deputy serving the warrant had been shot dead. I would be taking his place.

"Ok Billy, let's get him sworn in; get a photographer up here."

Within minutes, the Sheriff, the Undersheriff, Billy, Mazie and the photographer were in the office. This was getting to be a pretty big production. At first, the Sheriff had me stand by the window and raise my right hand. The photographer was lining up his shot of the sheriff and me with my right hand raised, but then the sheriff said,

"No, no, let's do it over by the flag."

We repositioned by the flag. I raised my right hand to take the oath of office. Just then a Deputy ran into the office.

"Sheriff, Sheriff, they just robbed the bank across the street."

"Oh my God," yelled the sheriff, "let's go."

Everybody ran out of the office leaving me standing by the flag with my right hand raised. After a short time, Mazie returned and said,

"You better come back tomorrow."

Eventually, I was sworn in and began working for Billy in the warrant squad. Billy was a highly regarded expert on civil and criminal law, and he was now my mentor. Every day he dealt with bench warrants, civil and criminal commitments, property seizures, and various orders of the court. The Sheriff was also in charge of the County Jail, and Billy acted as a liaison between the courts, law enforcement agencies, and the jail.

The jail housed prisoners, newly arrested, who had not yet been found guilty of a crime. Prisoners were charged with crimes that ranged from petty misdemeanors to murder and bank robbery. The jail also housed civil prisoners and Federal Witnesses. The Federal Witnesses usually had a bounty on their head and were therefore held under assumed names pending their testimony at high profile trials. Federal Witnesses were held apart from the normal jail population to preserve their anonymity. This was actually a money maker for the sheriff because the Federal Government paid well to keep these prisoners safe.

The history of the Sheriff's Department dated back to the colonial period. The first appointed sheriff in Westchester County was Thomas Pell in 1683, making it the earliest sheriff's Department established in what would become the United States.

Billy was taking care to educate me on the legal system and keep me out of harm's way. Despite the special treatment, I was accepted by other members of the squad because they did not view me as a threat. I don't think they expected me to be around for very long, and as it turned out, they were right.

There was talk of big political changes coming to the county. One plan under review was the formation of a Department of Correction. Next to the Jail was a County Penitentiary which was administered by the County Welfare Department. The plan involved merging the Sheriff's Jail and the penitentiary into a new Department of Correction under a Correction Commissioner. There was even talk of eliminating the position of Sheriff altogether or at least severely diminishing the position.

Billy could see the writing on the wall. He was getting ready to retire, but he would ride it out until it became untenable for him. As for me, Billy suggested I transfer to the Jail.

"That is the future," he would say. "Things are going to open up for those who can take advantage of it, and you need to be there."

On a Monday morning at seven o'clock I reported to the Jail for the first time. My work in the warrant squad was always in civilian clothes but now I would work in uniform. The County Jail was on a six-hundred-acre plot of county-owned land, which was mostly undeveloped. It did contain, however, the penitentiary, a hospital, and a senior living facility, as well as the jail. There were also residences for nurses and other professionals.

The jail looked ominous and impressive at the same time. Built in 1932, it was a sturdy structure of stone and mortar with huge front doors made of wood and strapped with iron. Sal Dario, wearing a white shirt bearing a gold badge on the left breast and captain bars on the collar, cracked the door and peered out at me.

"What do you want?" he said.

I held up my credentials, "Hi, I'm Deputy Sheriff Kenney, I start work here today."

Captain Dario opened the door wider so I could enter revealing the 38- caliber revolver he held in his right hand.

"Expecting someone else?" I asked.

Entry to the jail was controlled by a vestibule system sometimes referred to as a mantrap. It required two individual officers to open and close two doors independently. Due to being extremely short-handed this day, Captain Dario was operating both doors himself, hence the extra precaution. This may or may not have been prudent, but it indicated a particular mindset I would find throughout jail operations. There were cowboys in this modern Sheriff's Department. I'd just met one.

Captain Dario was a middle-aged man of tall but slight build. He was extremely competent and highly regarded by those who worked for him, eventually including me. He immediately became the next to steer me in directions I had no idea existed. Some proved to be not so great.

The Sheriff's Department provided no formal training of any kind. There was no academy, no firearms training, just on the job training. When I started work at the Warrant squad, I was issued no uniform or firearm. As a sworn peace officer, I was authorized to carry a sidearm, so you just went out and bought one. On this day in 1968, I did not carry my firearm and had not yet been issued a uniform.

Today was the day I would put on my "Cowboy" persona. A Cowboy persona, in this context, is someone who is reckless and does not have a suitable plan or understand the consequences of their actions. Or, a Cowboy can simply be unorthodox, going against the grain with a plan that he knows will have severe consequences should it fail. In the jail you must learn the first and grow into the second. The jail was Dodge City.

All shifts at the jail were short personnel, but, on this day, staff illnesses made it even worse than usual. The first floor of the jail prisoner housing area was a two-man post, but today only one Deputy was posted due to shortages. Captain Dario assigned me to work with Jimmy White on the first floor as a trainee. Jimmy explained to me that we worked from a desk in the main corridor that overlooked two dayrooms. There were 30 cells in the east cell block and 30 cells in the west cell block. The prisoners would eat breakfast in their cells, and after cleanup, they would be allowed into the dayrooms to watch TV, play cards, or just hang out. Jimmy would take the east cell block, and I would take the west.

I got a quick tour and then the west cell block was my responsibility for the rest of the day. Jimmy explained that the first thing we had to do was pick up "Prisoner Request Forms" and verify the prisoner count. The forms were filled out and placed on the prisoner's cell bars first thing in the morning. It was how a prisoner could request a phone call, see the doctor, or communicate with the shift captain. I went to my cell block and found forms uniformly placed on cell bars of about 20 cells. As I made my rounds picking up forms, I also counted each prisoner. Presenting the pile of forms to Jimmy, he explained.

"This is very important, make sure all forms are signed by the Prisoner with the proper cell number. Then place the pile of forms in this corner of the desk."

Jimmy carefully lined up the forms on the corner of the desk.

Jimmy stated, "The Captain will be back soon to collect these on each floor and verify our prisoner count."

I gave Jimmy my count of prisoners which he verified on a master sheet of names and cell numbers.

Captain Dario returned a few moments later and pondered the prisoner counts we had verified. Satisfied with the prisoner count he turned his attention to the stack of prisoner requests. He picked them up, looked through them quickly, then tore them in half and threw them into a waste basket. He headed to the elevator on his way to visit the other floors but suddenly turned and said to Jimmy,

"Explain to him why I did that."

Captain Dario then disappeared onto the elevator. I turned to Jimmy for an explanation of why the request slips were torn up and thrown away.

Jimmy shrugged, "I don't know, he does the same thing every morning."

The prisoners were allowed into the dayrooms once they had breakfast. One officer could watch 60 prisoners from the main corridor vantage point. Captain Dario called me out front. He explained that he had a prisoner who had to be taken to the hospital for a clinic appointment.

"Have you ever transported a prisoner?"

"Yeah," I replied. "Once."

"Just once," he repeated. "How far?"

"About six thousand miles."

"Oh."

A few hours into my employment at the Jail a prisoner was brought out to me in leg irons and handcuffs. Captain Dario then appeared with that same snub nosed 38 caliber revolver. In front of the prisoner, and I think mainly for the prisoner's benefit, the captain said,

"Have you ever handled a revolver?"

Then without waiting for my reply, he said, "The bullets go in here," pointing to the open cylinder.

"Then they come out here," he said, pointing to the end of the barrel.

"If he tries to escape, shoot him."

"I don't have a holster so load it and put it in your pocket."

And so began the first day of 25 years that I spent in jail.

I managed the prisoner transport without incident and upon returning to the jail the captain was still straining to get things done.

"Can you type?" he asked.

"Yeah, sure."

I'd learned to type in the military when assigned to the Master at Arms Force for a short time. Some of the processes at the Jail were archaic and over burdening, especially considering the shortage of staff.

One example was a very long form onto which 300 prisoners' names had to be typed once per shift. It was a cell locator for prisoners. During each shift, new prisoners' names were penciled in, and discharged prisoners were scratched off. Some prisoners would be transferred within the jail. It was a working form, and at the end of the shift, it was ready to be re-typed for the next shift to work off of.

I was busy typing when Captain Gannon of the three to eleven shift walked in. Captain Gannon was not tall, but he was huge. A man in his fifties, his hand swallowed mine when introduced. The two Captains were now face to face with Gannon speaking first.

"The new man is not going on the day shift, Sal. I need him on the three to eleven shift, and he can type."

They seemed to be fighting over me when they left the room, presumably to seek guidance from higher authority. When they returned Captain Gannon notified me that I was to report to the three to eleven shift the next day. The day shift was going off duty, but I agreed to stay and finish typing the prisoner cell location form. Captain Gannon moved slowly, spoke carefully, and was African American. All three characteristics are important to the story.

The majority of jail staff were white while the majority of prisoners were black. I would have to say there was a general lack of understanding between the two groups, but the white guys were in charge. Today, this would be a diversity problem. However, the jail was a very violent place, and it was my experience that staff was just as quick to beat the hell out of a white guy as they were a black one. Rarely did a day go by that I wasn't wrestling (the nice word), or fighting, (the more accurate one), with someone. Usually, it was three or four Deputies against one prisoner. Sometimes that was justified and sometimes it was not. The problem was there was no one overseeing our response so there were never consequences.

Prisoners coming into the jail, for the most part, were newly arrested. Prisoners were committed, drunk, high on drugs, psychotic, covered in blood, with gunshot wounds, broken bones, looking to escape or take revenge on anyone. Maybe our latest guest had been standing over his dead wife with a bloody knife in his hand a few hours ago. We strip-search him, book him by asking a lot of questions, and possibly antagonize him unintentionally.

"Who is your next of kin?"

The brother he just killed.

"What is your address?"

"You mean the house I just burned down."

It's happened.

Then, of course, is the interaction among inmates on the cell block. Fights were common, usually with makeshift weapons readily available, like a chair or a knife fashioned from a toothbrush. Something as simple as a pencil could be a dangerous weapon. A new prisoner on the block with clean sneakers would suffer a beating and loss of his footwear. I had seen prisoners beaten for their underwear. Surviving is simple- you must be the one stealing the underwear, not the one giving it up.

A deputy could be in charge of up to sixty prisoners, distributed in cell blocks of up to fifteen prisoners each. Fifteen individual cells were located within one large cell that the deputy patrolled. He had visibility of all cells and prisoners but was protected by the bars of the larger cell. There were times during the movement of prisoners when a lone deputy could be exposed to thirty prisoners. Dayrooms containing up to thirty prisoners was one of the more dangerous places.

Sometimes, prisoners acted alone to do bad things. Sometimes, they conspired in groups to hurt someone, steal something, or escape. On occasion, they acted en masse to riot, protest, or simply fight the system. The jail as an entity, had a personality. An experienced officer could feel tension, trouble brewing. silence, noise, both contribute to the climate. How about the full moon? Speaking from twenty-five years of experience, yeah, the full moon was often a time of trouble.

Captain Gannon assigned me to the first floor with a senior deputy. We were responsible for 60 prisoners. Two dayrooms held 30 prisoners each that we could observe from our desk. There were wall phones strategically placed. Dial 4, hang up and it would register on a tape that you were at that location at that time of day. Dial 9 and an alarm would sound, resulting in the crash crew responding, prepared for anything. To get the same response, break the phone, pull the cord out, or just leave it off the hook, and the alarm would sound. While we called them the Crash Crew, the prisoners called them the Goon Squad. In actuality, it was more like melding Seal Team 6 and "The Village People." You have to think about that one for a while but it's pretty accurate.

Shortly after shift change, Captain Gannon would come into the back section of the jail. His deep, booming voice would call out .

"Everything ah'right?"

"It's all good Cap".

He would then laugh, maybe it was a nervous laugh because nothing funny was said. Then, he would often say,

"Kenney, come with me."

We would get on one of two elevators and go to the third floor. One elevator had to be on the first floor at all times for use by the Crash Crew. I was never sure if I was Captain Gannons' bodyguard or if he was grooming me for something. Whatever the intent, I learned how the man operated, and it inspired my own conduct with prisoners.

The quality that impressed me about Captain Gannon was that all prisoners respected him. He would talk to anyone and everyone. He would accept written requests from anyone. He would always try to resolve violence in a peaceful manner. Because of this, he was looked upon as weak by many, including the administration of the jail. But I admired Captain Gannon for his strength that others could not see.

The jail was known as a dumping ground for the Sheriff. If he felt someone was incompetent, he sent them to the jail. If he had to appoint someone as a political favor, they went to the jail. I was at first viewed as the latter, and I guess I was. I realized early on that I had to prove myself, and I worked hard to do that. In the office I proved my worth as a typist, booking inmates into the jail faster than most. I could handle the books involving petty cash and prisoner money.

Money had to be reconciled at the end of every shift. This was complicated by prisoner money taken at booking and returned upon transfer or release. The jail, on average, booked twenty to thirty new prisoners every shift and transferred or released as many. Cash bail, which at times could be in the tens of thousands of dollars, had to be documented and safeguarded. I've seen more than one paper bag filled with a hundred thousand dollars in cash. I helped Captain Gannon out many times when things just didn't add up.

Every prisoner committed to the jail had to be accompanied by the proper legal documents. The most common were Local Jurisdiction Criminal Commitments which had to be signed by a judge, but there were also Federal, Civil, Material Witness, and Bail Bondsman commitments that had to be carefully scrutinized for legality. Some of these documents were complicated and contained multiple pages. If one accepts a prisoner on documents that did not meet the legal standard, the crime of unlawful imprisonment could be charged.

The time I spent with Billy McNeil of the warrant squad proved invaluable. He taught me two practices that stayed with me for my entire career. First, when a legal document was received, it could contain many pages.

"Don't go by the first page summary. Read every page and understand it."

Second, "you can't know every legal situation you may run into, but you can know someone who does."

Even more important than your own knowledge was cultivating relationships with people you can call upon.

I proved my abilities working in the jail's administrative areas and the cell blocks. I was able to get through most days without major problems. I took care of small problems without bothering the captain. That was something noticed and appreciated.

When force was required, it was known that I could be counted on. I became part of the so-called "Goon Squad". I was always assigned to the first floor, so if an alarm sounded on the second or third floors when the crash crew responded I would join them and respond to the alarm with them. Responding to an alarm was always suspenseful. The responding three to five officers often did not know if they would confront a single prisoner or thirty.

Another common problem was prisoners refusing to go to court or leave their cell. The use of too many officers to extract a prisoner usually amounted to one or more of them being injured. Everything in a cell is hard steel with sharp corners and edges to fall against or be pushed into. I eventually teamed up with a small, wiry officer named Willy Simone.

On one occasion, because of shortages, just the two of us were tasked with getting a prisoner out of his cell. On the way to the cell Willy said,

"You go in high, and I'll go in low".

The prisoner was backed against the wall, ready to fight. Willy went in low, grabbing him around the legs while I went over the top of Willy, wrestling the prisoner to the ground. We got him face down, handcuffed behind his back and marched out of the cell in short order. No one was injured and this scenario was repeated numerous times with the two of us as a team.

With my reputation spreading, I was naturally assigned to the Sheriff's Riot Squad. At first, it was just practicing tactics once a month. The one and only time we were called to action was when Martin Luther King was assassinated and Peekskill, New York erupted in riot. Peekskill was about a half-hour ride from the Jail. There were about twenty of us in a car and van speeding up the highway. Trying to cut the tension, we were joking around in the van, and I was mocking and imitating the Sheriff.

"This is the Sheriff, throw down your guns," I said in a gruff voice.

Everyone in the van was laughing. Little did I realize I was sitting on the microphone and had depressed the button broadcasting my voice. The next transmission that came over the radio was.

"This is the Sheriff, and you are not funny, Kenney."

We made the rest of the trip in dead silence.

Once we entered Peekskill, we headed toward the police department. The streets were bare, but most of the businesses we passed had smashed windows, and countless burglar alarms could be heard. Sirens sounded in the background and small fires dotted the streets. The sheriff had committed us to assist the Peekskill Police Department at their request. I entered the police department with Captain Dario to check in with the Police Chief. We found him sitting at his desk unable to function. Captain Dario walked over and patted him on the back.

"Don't worry Chief, we'll get your town back for you."

With that, we left and drove around looking for a mission.

Driving through the main business district, we could see about a block ahead of us that the road was barricaded by a large group. Tires were on fire, and the sound of burglar alarms and sirens was constant. The barricaded group seemed to be taunting the few Police Officers present.

We offloaded and formed a tactical "V" shape across the road. I was the point of the "V," as we'd practiced once or twice. The plan was to march forward penetrate the barricade and rout the agitators. Being at the head of the formation, I could not see deputies to my left and right. Our uniform consisted of a helmet with a face shield, a firearm and long wooden riot baton held at port arms. I heard the command "Forward" and began my methodical march toward the barricade about fifty yards away. Getting closer to the barricaded group I could see the look of astonishment on their faces. Then I heard in the distance,

"Fred..... Fred."

I turned around, and to my horror, I was alone. After the command forward, the squad had been ordered to halt, but I had not heard the command and continued my assault on the barricade. I can't imagine what the group of protesters may have thought of one lone Deputy Sheriff marching down the street toward them. I very slowly backtracked to safety. For reasons unknown, we returned to the police department, where we waited for a couple of hours before being told we were not needed any longer.

Chapter 4

THE GRAND JURY

Rumors continued to circulate that a new Department of Correction was being formed. The Sheriff's jail, the adjacent penitentiary, and a future women's prison would be combined under new leadership. Most of the jail staff were not happy with this possibility and wanted to remain Deputy Sheriffs.

Some deputies wanted to transfer out of the jail to remain with the sheriff in the event this change came about. The day shift staff feared Captain Dario would be one of those leaving. Notwithstanding some of his "Cowboy" methods, he supported his staff, and when problems arose, he confronted them head-on. That was one of the problems at the jail. The shift captain made the rules as needed for a given situation. There were no rules or procedures one could refer to or violate.

The jail was Dodge City, the deputies were the posse, and the shift captain was Marshall Dillon. That will only make sense if you are old enough to remember Gunsmoke.

Captain Dario ruled over the day shift. Some of his methods were unconventional, but compared to what? It was almost an impossible task. The jail served forty-four local police jurisdictions, plus state and federal law enforcement. The shift was always short of staff.

Police cars were backed up outside the jail with prisoners waiting to be committed. A time-consuming booking form had to be typed for each prisoner admitted. Numerous prisoners were scheduled to be in County Court, some had hospital clinic appointments. There was a fire in C block, a fight in B block. The current prisoner being booked was high on drugs, refusing to cooperate, and there were twenty more in the bullpen who were starting to get unruly due to the crowded, sweltering conditions. That could describe a typical shift at the jail.

It was all in a day's work for the captain and his loyal deputies. They were accustomed to the daily chaos. I was accustomed to the military way of doing things. By the book. The jail had no book.

I contributed where I could. I came up with a system to replace the prisoner cell locator form that took hours to type every shift. I replaced it with a simple name card and slot system. Type the prisoners name on a card and place it into the slot for that cell. Pull the card if the prisoner was discharged or transferred. It was always up to date and required no extra work. When I suggested this system to Captain Dario, he implemented it immediately.

When a prisoner was sentenced, he had to be given credit for "jail time". I would see a records officer counting on his fingers how many days left in January, then how many days in February this year. I again came up with a simpler system that was immediately adopted. Instead of going by months, every day of the year has a number 1 through 365. From there, simple math would tell you how many days a prisoner spent in jail.

My contributions were being noticed. I no longer worked on the cell blocks; I was usually assigned to the booking office and record keeping. I was also picking up some of the captain's responsibilities, freeing him to get more done.

As a parting gesture, the Sheriff dumped a few more of his least favored deputies onto the jail payroll. This extra help was needed, but the quality was poor.

The only way to get into the Sheriff's Department was to be appointed by the Sheriff. There was no test, no requirements, other than having a "Rabbi" (someone to speak up for you). Early on, I worked with and for some very competent professionals. When I arrived at the jail, those in charge were trying to get better training and working conditions. They were trying to weed out, or at least improve the performance of, some of the less competent deputies. Some of the so called political appointed deputies were not capable of dealing with the violent criminal element. Mistakes can be deadly.

Deputy Sheriff Thomas Franklyn was one such individual who was transferred to the jail payroll. Supervisors had little faith in his abilities, resulting in him getting easy assignments. On this day, due to a shortage of staff, Deputy Sheriff Franklyn was assigned to escort prisoner Richard Fisher to the hospital for a clinic appointment.

Fisher was awaiting trial for armed robbery. He was twenty-eight years old, six feet tall, two hundred pounds. Franklyn was five foot eight, one hundred fifty pounds. Fisher had the weight and the height, but Franklyn had the gun. In most cases the guy with the gun wins.

Following protocol, the prisoner was strip searched and put into an orange jumpsuit. He was handcuffed with a chain around his waist, holding the handcuffs tight against his body. The chain was padlocked, and he was placed in leg irons. Deputy Sheriff Franklyn was armed with a 38-caliber revolver.

The Deputy and his prisoner were conspicuous in the clinic area of the hospital. They caught the attention of an off-duty police officer present on a personal matter.

Moments after passing and noting the prisoner, Patrolman John Hilliard heard yelling and a commotion in a room behind him. He turned and ran back the way he had come. Arriving at the doorway, he observed Deputy Sheriff Franklyn on his back, straddled by prisoner Richard Fisher. Fisher had Franklyn's gun in his hand with the muzzle pressed firmly against the Deputy's head.

Officer Hilliard drew his own weapon and fired twice, hitting and killing Richard Fisher. Deputy Sheriff Franklyn was uninjured physically, but the experience left him too shaken to continue employment. Patrolman Hilliard was rightly recognized for his heroic actions. Deputy Franklyn found one of the bullets that killed Fisher in his upper left shirt pocket after the incident. This was just a fluke. The bullet, after passing through Fishers' body, fell harmlessly into Franklyns' pocket. Deputy Sheriff Franklyn was a nice man but not cut out for this job.

Violence in all forms plagued the jail. Escape attempts, fights, and mayhem were all too common. Disruption to the system manifests in many different forms. There was no routine day and some days were truly chaotic.

C block on the second floor of the jail contained twelve prisoners who had begun a food protest over various ever-changing complaints. First it was about the food, but the protest quickly morphed to cover problems with the courts, confinement, and their general malaise with the system. They were kept in their cells and denied dayroom privileges due to their unruly behavior.

On day one of their protest, breakfast was served on aluminum trays and consisted of milk, cereal, and toast. Each prisoner stood at the front of his cell and, in unison, threw the tray and food onto the corridor floor. Prisoner "trustees" reluctantly cleaned up the mess. Trustees are prisoners who are afforded privileges or a small stipend to clean common areas in the cell blocks. Food was also thrown at lunch and dinner meals. The trustees refused to clean up the resulting mess for fear of retaliation from other prisoners sympathetic to the demonstrators. The area was quickly becoming a health hazard.

As this protest went into the second day, jail officials reasoned the prisoners would soon get hungry and give up the protest. However, deputies on the cell block were aware prisoners were eating some of the food and had been stockpiling other snacks in preparation for their protest.

Prisoners are allowed to make purchases from the commissary containing snack items and toiletries. Prior to the protest, prisoners had stockpiled purchased items in preparation for the planned demonstration.

It would appear there was no end in sight to the disruption. Breakfast on the third day resulted in the same mess, but lunch presented a new wrinkle.

Instead of throwing the food and aluminum tray out onto the corridor in front of the cells, the prisoners retained the aluminum tray and only threw the food. The aluminum tray was then used to bang on the bars in unison in an endless tumultuous disturbance that could be heard in the penitentiary next door.

There was fear that the protest would spread further, to other cell blocks or to the penitentiary.

When I reported to work at three that afternoon, I was informed a plan had been formulated to end the protest. Captain Dario was waiting for the evening shift to relieve his day shift. Then he, along with his entire day shift, would put an end to the prisoner protest. Captain Dario pointed at me,

"Fred, you're with us."

I could see Captain Gannon was concerned about the plan. Captain Sal Dario had a reputation of dealing with this sort of thing using "overwhelming escalation". Just take your response to a level your opposition can't or is not willing to go.

"Sal, I'll go up and talk to them again, see if we can end this peacefully," said Captain Gannon.

"Enough talk, who is running this place, us or the prisoners? Let's go."

Captain Dario led his shift to the elevators with me trailing apprehensively behind. I respected Captain Gannon and agreed one last effort to end the rebellion without violence would have been reasonable.

I had no frame of reference to prepare me for what would come next. This would be the first such situation I'd be involved in. Captain Dario divided his shift into three four-person teams. I was the odd man, mainly left to observe and jump in as needed.

There was no conversation with the prisoners upon arrival on the cell block. Four officers lined up in front of each cell; the cell door sprung open, and the officers rushed in quickly, overpowering each inmate with brute force. The slightest resistance resulted in a flurry of punches and kicks with no regard for the resulting injuries.

The prisoner was stripped, handcuffed, and the cell contents thrown onto the corridor with no concern for the destruction of personal property. Virtually everything was destroyed. The prisoner, naked, was returned to his cell devoid of all comfort. The next prisoner in line, knowing what was coming, attempted to defend himself only to find that provoked a more violent response.

The entire operation took under two hours and resulted in twelve naked prisoners in steel cells devoid of any comfort items, mattresses, or blankets. All personal property lay destroyed on the ground and was deposited in bags for disposal.

The operation was a success, with everyone apparently comfortable with the results. Everyone except me. I was in disbelief at what I had witnessed. Some of the prisoners had injuries, and all were naked. Captain Dario and his crew left the area satisfied the problem had been resolved. I could not imagine there would be no repercussions for such an unreasonable, likely unlawful, act.

Captain Dario "briefed" Captain Gannon indicating the protest was over and then went off duty with the day shift. Captain Gannon was left with an impossible situation. I was horrified by what I had just taken part in. I expected a thoughtful, experienced approach rather than the reckless, damn-the-consequences scene I had just witnessed. Captain Gannon took me with him to check on the prisoners. When we got to the cell block and observed the condition the prisoners were in, Captain Gannon turned to face me,

"What the fuck did he do?"

I didn't answer, no explanation from me could explain better than the reality in front of us.

Four inmates required trips to the emergency room, one with a broken jaw. Captain Gannon ordered jail clothing, mattresses, and bedding to be returned to all prisoners. Captain Gannon, as usual, got respect and cooperation. He allowed some prisoners to take showers one at a time, which had not been allowed for several days. He allowed some to make phone calls, understanding the consequences that might result from that communication.

We were shorthanded as usual but managed to get the four prisoners to the emergency room one at a time over the next several hours. Captain Gannon notified the Jail Warden, who at the time was the Undersheriff. He had to cover his ass; he knew this would not be swept under the rug.

I received a call from Captain Dario at my home the following day.

"We have to get our stories straight because Captain Gannon ratted us out. There's going to be a big investigation."

I couldn't help but think, 'What did you expect would happen?'

The headline, front page of the local paper read: COUNTY JAIL MELEE. A grand jury was convened to investigate and possibly level criminal charges against participants. Captain Dario made it clear to me and the rest of his crew that our story had to be consistent with his report.

His report stated in attempting to quell a riot by the named prisoners, officers were met with force and objects were thrown, requiring Staff to defend themselves. Perjury is a crime, and I was being told I had to agree with a report I knew to be false.

I was not happy with the situation I had been placed in, but at that point, I could see no good way out. There would be no future for me in this department if I went against Captain Dario and his wolfpack. But if I supported his narrative, I would commit the crime of perjury and go against my personal values.

I had heard stories about "elevator rides" where a problem prisoner would be removed from his cell and transferred to a different floor. The elevator would stop between floors, and the prisoner would receive a beating. I had dismissed them as mere rumors, but I had no doubt now that those stories were true. Captain Dario likely was the architect of some of the more misguided happenings in the jail.

Within a week, everyone had received a Grand Jury Subpoena to testify regarding the incident. Captain Gannon and Captain Dario were among the first to testify. I am told that Captain Gannon replied, "I don't recall," over 20 times to questions put to him. Captain Gannon did not agree with the tactics employed, but he could not or would not go against Captain Dario.

Captain Dario stuck to his story, as did the day shift officers. Finally, I was scheduled to testify. Captain Dario called me at home advising me not to wear the combat-type boots most deputies wear because one prisoner testified that he had been kicked by an officer wearing combat boots.

I was sitting in the Grand Jury waiting room. The Assistant District Attorney presenting the case told me he would be calling me before the Grand Jury momentarily. I had already signed a "Waiver of Immunity", which was a requirement of my employment. Law enforcement officers generally have partial immunity from civil or criminal liability while performing official duties. However, it was the position of the County Legal Department that employees under investigation should voluntarily waive their right to immunity as a condition of employment. Employees could not be compelled to waive immunity, but failing to comply would be cause for termination.

I was conflicted and trying to figure out how I might respond to questions before the grand jury. I knew sticking to the false story would be in my personal best interest, but I did not want to be untruthful. As I waited nervously, the outer corridor door opened, and an attorney stepped in.

Looking around, he casually said, "I'm looking for my client..."

Then he took a double take at me. "Hey Fred, what are you doing here?"

The Attorney was Joel Jacobs, who I knew well from his visits to the jail. He visited his clients at the jail in the early evening. He would often come into the booking office to get information, and I always helped him out as much as I could. Sometimes, he would drop in just to say hello. Joel was brilliant and was practicing what I had been taught by Billy McNeil. Cultivate those with knowledge you may someday need. I replied to Joel's question by telling him about the alleged riot.

"Are you involved in that?" he asked.

"Yeah, I'm right in the middle of it."

Just then, the Assistant District Attorney poked his head in from the other door leading to the grand jury room.

"OK, Mr. Kenney, we're ready for you."

I was about to get up when Joel interrupted.

"I'm Joel Jacobs, attorney of record for Mr. Kenney. He is not testifying today. Fred, come on, let's go."

I looked at the District Attorney, who just stared back with a blank expression.

"Let's go, Fred," Joel repeated.

I got up without looking at the District Attorney and departed with Joel. As I left the room, the protest I expected to hear behind me did not materialize.

I never did testify, and the Grand Jury returned a judgement of "No True Bill", meaning no criminal charges were filed. Instead, the Grand Jury issued a report critical of management. It offered suggestions on how situations should be handled in the future.

Their recommendations were not binding and were not considered by anyone at the jail.

Captain Dario was a complicated individual. Aside from being unpredictable, he was very competent. He knew the law, particularly as it applied to the jail and prisoners. His shift ran efficiently despite shortages and emergencies. Every officer had the deepest respect for him, including me. No matter what, he was there for his men. He could be compassionate with staff and prisoners but don't provoke him. He was ruthless when angered, and he was quick to anger.

The new Department of Correction came to pass with an appropriate budget, additional staff, and accountability. The Penitentiary held prisoners sentenced for misdemeanor crimes up to one year in length. The prisoner would receive credit for any time spent incarcerated before the sentence and Good Behavior Time up to one-third of the sentence.

Sentenced prisoners knew when they would be released, relieving much of the anxiety. All told, the penitentiary was a more relaxed environment for prisoners and employees. That didn't mean things could not go wrong. Quite often, they did. When things went sideways, staff and prisoners faced the same dangers one might expect at the jail. The problem was in the mindset of the staff at the penitentiary. Guards, and even the Penitentiary Administration, did not operate with a maximum-security mindset. They were not prepared for the worst when it did occur.

The jail was maximum security due to the nature of prisoners admitted. Jail prisoners most often have no idea if they will ever get out. The prisoner was still processing the crime committed, resulting arrest, and possible consequences. That uncertainty made prisoners inherently volatile. In the jail you never knew where the danger would come from. You just knew it was coming.

Transfers of prisoners between the jail and Penitentiary were commonplace. A jail prisoner might be sentenced to misdemeanor time in the Penitentiary and transfer. Similarly, a penitentiary prisoner may have a felony warrant lodged against him, in which case, he would be transferred to the Jail upon completion of his sentence. As feared the penitentiary lacked the appropriate security philosophy. Penitentiary staff did not adapt well at the jail and jail staff quite often had to solve penitentiary shortcomings.

Captain Dario received a call from the penitentiary that a prisoner who was to be transferred to the jail was refusing to leave his cell and was threatening to set fire to it. Captain Dario yelled into the phone,

"What the hell do you want me to do about it?"

After more conversation, he slammed the phone down.

"Fred, you and Willy go over to the Penitentiary and get this fucking guy threatening to set a fire and refusing to leave his cell. Jesus, they can't do a fucking thing over there."

A tunnel connected the two buildings. The penitentiary prepared all the food for the jail, so there was already a working relationship between the two.

Willy and I arrived in the penitentiary and were directed to the third floor of C Block. We found five or six officers and the shift captain milling around, unwilling or unable to deal with one prisoner.

I was advised that the prisoner was in the last cell. Without hesitation, I told the officer operating the lock box to spring the door as soon as we reached it. Willy and I made our way down the cellblock, and as we reached the door, it sprung open.

Neither of us knew the prisoner or what to expect, but we had done this numerous times. We entered the cell almost simultaneously, Willy slightly ahead of me and going low. Surprising the prisoner, he offered little resistance as we placed him face down on the floor and handcuffed him.

We were in the cell for maybe thirty seconds. We brought him to his feet with Willy holding one arm and me on the other. The look of amazement on the faces of the penitentiary officers and the captain as we marched him out of the cell was well worth the trip.

One of the greatest dangers in any jail is fire. Made of steel and stone, the structure itself offers little to burn. However, mattresses were necessary, and they burned with acrid black smoke that quickly accumulates in cell blocks devoid of cross ventilation. Prisoners locked in individual cells take time to be freed while smoke travels fast. In a majority of prison fires where death occurs it is the smoke not the fire that poses the greatest danger.

Companies advertised "Fire Retardant" mattresses for prisons, but that only referred to the outer covering. Once the outer cover was breached, the flammable material inside poses a fire danger. When we think of a mass murderer, an active shooter comes to mind. Therefore, the thinking goes, if we ban all guns, we can stop mass murder. Not really. Some of the worst mass murderers used fire as their weapon of choice. I have had the misfortune of knowing some of them.

Thomas Ruppert had been in the jail for almost two years before I began employment. Ruppert had been charged with twelve counts of first-degree murder in the arson death of nine adults and three children when he was just sixteen years old. At the time of the murders, Ruppert had been employed part-time in a Jewish Community Center in Yonkers, New York. A suspicious fire at the center killed twelve people.

From the beginning of the investigation, Ruppert was the prime suspect.

Ruppert eventually confessed his crime to the director of the community center and subsequently to the police. In 1967, at eighteen years of age, he was found guilty of twelve counts of first-degree murder and sentenced to twelve life sentences.

The sentencing judge said he felt sorry for Ruppert due to his age and wished he could have convicted him as a youthful offender. A youthful offender conviction would have made him eligible for release at twenty-one years of age. However, due to the seriousness of this case, life sentences were mandatory. In May 1970, the conviction was reversed because it was ruled that both the confession to the director of the community center and the confession to the police were tainted. A new trial was ordered, but without the confessions as evidence a conviction was impossible.

On June 11, 1971, Thomas Alfred Ruppert walked out of the County Jail a free man, only to lead a short life and pass away at the age of thirty-five.

I also recall a time when an alarm went off on the second floor of the jail about mid-day. Responding officers found prisoner Peter Leonard crying in his cell and bleeding from slashed wrists. He was brought to the front administration section of the jail, awaiting transportation to the hospital. Just a few days ago, in July 1974, Peter Leonard had been committed to the County Jail charged with twenty-six counts of first-degree murder.

He had intentionally set fire to a bowling alley and the attached Gulliver's Tavern, where 26 young revelers died trying to escape the fire and smoke. Countless others were injured, some seriously, including thirteen firefighters. Leonard had burglarized the bowling alley and set fire to it in a desperate attempt to cover up his crime. The fire spread quickly, trapping and killing 26 people in the attached tavern.

He sat on a wooden bench in the front hallway of the jail, crying and screaming intermittently that he wanted to die. He prominently displayed his bloodied wrists palm up. Captain Dario walked over to examine his injuries. Wiping the blood from his wrists, the captain found the wounds to be superficial.

Captain Dario stood menacingly over Leonard.

"Do you really want to die?"

Other officers were gathered around tightly. This was quickly turning into a sideshow with Captain Dario the ringmaster.

"If you really want to die-!" he shouted as he reached into his pocket, withdrawing a knife and holding it high overhead. He triggered the switchblade mechanism, causing a silver blade to spring forth locking into place with a metallic click. His arm arced down, slamming the point of the knife into the wooden bench inches from Leonard. It stuck like an arrow.

The captain shouted at the whimpering form stretched out before him.

"If you really want to die, take that and cut your fucking throat. Do something right for once in your sorry fucking life."

Leonard slid off the bench onto the floor, screaming louder than before.

Leonard's wounds required no sutures; he was patched up at the hospital and returned to his cell with bandaged wrists. He wasn't finished causing problems, and his next transgression nearly cost more lives. Two weeks later, Leonard set fire to two mattresses in his cell in an apparent suicide attempt with little regard for the other twenty inmates in his cell block.

When I arrived on the cell block, thick black smoke poured from the area of Leonard's cell. The smoke was quickly spreading throughout the block. The twenty prisoners locked in cells would suffocate within minutes. Visibility in the cell block was near zero as officers raced against time to free all the prisoners. They were initially evacuated to an adjoining dayroom but had to be moved again as the smoke spread.

An officer found the unconscious Leonard by feeling his way to the cell, then dragged him to safety. Leonard was again transported to the hospital, this time for smoke inhalation and burns. Several Correction Officers were also treated for smoke related illness. The fire was small and quickly extinguished, but the smoke lingered for days. If not for the heroic actions of officers, Leonard and possibly others would have perished.

Leonard pleaded guilty just before his trial was to start on June 16, 1975, and was sentenced to fifteen years to life in prison. On July 17, 1977, his conviction was overturned on a technicality. He was retried and found guilty by a jury on September 17, 1978. That verdict was again overturned, and yet another trial was ordered. On April 9, 1986, Leonard pleaded guilty to manslaughter and was sentenced to 15 years in prison, making him almost immediately eligible for parole.

In December 1980, Luis Marin was committed to the County Jail, where I first met him. He was charged with 26 counts of first-degree murder. He was a 26-year-old Guatemalan working as a busboy at the Stouffers Inn in Harrison, NY. He had been working under an assumed name and had just been informed that he was to be let go because of his immigration status.

It was charged in an indictment that he set fire to the Conference Center at the Stouffers Inn, where executives from all over the country were in attendance. The Conference Center due to its size hosted simultaneous events for prominent corporations. There were over one hundred attendees from some of the largest corporations in America. Some survivors had to jump from third floor windows to escape the smoke and flames. Many did not escape. The fire started on the third floor at the apex of two main corridors. Marin had been working in that same area with sterno cans to keep coffee hot just before the fire. Marin told investigators several contradictory stories about his actions during and after the fire. According to investigators, Marin gave the appearance or impression of guilt when being questioned.

In 1982, Jurors took six days of deliberations to find him guilty on all charges. He faced twenty-six life sentences upon sentencing. Marin would never serve his sentence. In an unprecedented decision, Judge Martin vacated the guilty verdict entered by the jury. Judge Martin said that the District Attorney convinced the jury to find him guilty with a brilliant summation but had not proven his case.

In his decision, the judge noted that countless witnesses had been called at trial, and much evidence had been produced, but none of the evidence tied Marin to the fire. Judge Martins's decision was upheld upon appeal. Luis Marin was a free man.

Those three cases stand out in my mind due to the horrific impact on innocents and the community at large. Each crime was the big news of the day, and one could not help being affected by the coverage. I was able to observe each prisoner over a protracted period and form my own out-of-court opinion as to culpability and remorse. It was my opinion that each of these offenders demonstrated a proclivity for committing the crimes charged and expressed no empathy for the many victims. Instead, each one was consumed with self-pity for the situation they languished in.

Chapter 5

FAST FREDDY, "I'M BACK."

It was a time in my life where I had a secure position with the Sheriff's Department. The pay was not great at the time, but I was getting by. I was proud both of my service in the Navy and the fact that I had followed in Grandpa George and Uncle Jerry's footsteps, continuing to serve my community in law enforcement. It appeared that life was complete, yet there was something lacking.

I thought about the old pool room, Popeye, Pete, and the culture surrounding them. I learned many life lessons in that pool room, and I missed the competition and the constant drive to be the best. But I had been away from the game for a long time and could not see a path back.

During my service in the Navy, I had limited time to play pool. Upon returning home, my focus shifted to more pressing matters like securing employment and contemplating the future. The familiar pool room had vanished, and my old friends had dispersed.

A chance encounter offered the impetus I needed to find my way back. I ran into Dan, an old friend from Popeye's pool room.

"Hey, Fred, you still playing pool?"

"Nah, I haven't played in a long time."

"Let's get together and play some."

I was surprised to find out Dan had become a fireman after I'd enlisted. Equally surprising to him was my job as a Deputy Sheriff. When I knew Dan, he didn't seem very motivated. Although, he might say the same about me.

The next day, we met at a nearby poolroom and played all afternoon. We told old stories about Popeye's Pool Room and had a good time catching up. I realized how much I missed the game, especially when I played better than expected.

Thanks to Dan, my interest and desire to play pool again was rekindled. As Fast Eddie Felson said in the movie, "Color of Money",

"I'm back."

As a teenager in Popeye's Poolroom, I fell in love with the game, the culture, the characters, and the money. More than anything, I think I enjoyed the recognition that came from being able to do something that most could not. I was a natural, and the game came to me quickly. I understood spin and deflection, draw, follow, and all the nuances of the game. I knew how to stay down on the shot and the concept of pocket speed. It wasn't just the game of pool that I loved, it was the feeling of being able to outplay everyone else that inspired me.

Pool rooms have always had a bad reputation. I know my mother panicked when she found out I was hanging out in a pool room. I can't say there weren't some fights and illegal activity, but I always felt safe. When you treat people with respect, you generally see it returned.

I've played in many poolrooms over the years, winning money from perfect strangers with never a problem. Case in point: Popeye's poolroom wasn't the only one in town. There was another pool room on the southside where white players did not venture. That is, until I decided to check it out.

Upon entering, every set of eyes flashed to me. I guess it had been a while since a white guy walked in. It was a little awkward at first, but I quickly got a game with a fellow named Rollo. 9 ball was not a popular game in this room. 8 ball was the game of choice for gambling.

8 ball was a game that can have varying rules, so I was careful to get the rules straight from the beginning. I didn't want any misunderstandings. I'd played 8 ball, and it was a popular game wherever you may play. The main difference was that only two players play 8 ball. 9 ball can have more than two players, which was called a "Ring Game". I may have been misguided but

I had no concern about my safety playing in this all black poolroom. There were some murmurings in the background about a "White Hustler" and a few other derogatory remarks, but that was it. Hustling in a strange pool room, white, black, or even Asian can cause some tension.

I won a few dollars before Rollo quit.

"You too good for me, bro," he said with a smile.

Rollo shook my hand, "You can come back any time, you won't have any problems here. Just tell them you're a friend of Rollo."

Poolrooms boast a unique cast of characters famously known by identifiers such as "Grady the Professor," "Tommy the Crab," "One-Eyed Mike," "Popeye", and others. Many of their stories would be worthy of their own memoir. Some of whom have skills that defy the laws of physics.

From the beginning, I observed skilled players closely. I watched their stance, how they stroked the ball, eye movement, head position. Among the great players, I found no common denominator. They all did it differently, or so it would seem. No matter how good your stroke or stance may be, all that matters was the fraction of a second when the tip of the cue stick was in contact with the cue ball, propelling it forward. No matter the method, if you do that right, you can be a winner.

I've seen many good players who could make the cue ball do impressive things to wow the crowds. There were a handful of great players who make the game look easy. The cue ball does nothing impressive. It hits the object ball cleanly into the pocket and gets in line for the next shot.

Popeye taught me hustling, "It's not how good you play; it's who you play."

Early on that was good advice. I could not afford to lose because I didn't have much money. However, I wanted to play better players. The good players had more money and they played for higher stakes. It was the incentive I needed to gradually overtake them.

If a player thought he had a chance to cash in on a big win, he would be more likely to gamble. Popeye taught me how to mimic the big roll of bills he always carried.

"Get yourself ten or twenty singles and then wrap them up with a ten or twenty dollar bill. Flash this roll, and you will get more games."

As I got older, this became twenties' wrapped up with a fifty. It worked just as well.

Popeye also taught me how to convincingly downplay my game to hide my true skill. I could always tell when a hustler was trying to hide his true speed. He would miss easy shots while playing skillful cue ball position. A skilled player can be measured not only by the shots he makes but also by the positioning of the cue ball. Popeye taught me to play position for a long difficult shot. Then, when I miss, well, it was a tough shot and doesn't arouse suspicion.

Pete, the counterman, steered me into the right games.

"Play this guy, don't play that guy."

Only a handful of strangers ever entered Popeyes Poolroom. If a stranger came up the long flight of stairs a lookout would alert Pete to hide all the racing sheets. That stranger was either an undercover cop looking to bust Popeye or a "Roadie", also known as a "Hustler", looking to relieve a pool player of his money.

One such "Roadie" was "Agusatee". He was Spanish, in his twenties, of slight build, and sporting a conspicuous mustache. He walked in carrying his two-piece cue stick without a case. After walking around the room, sizing everyone up, he approached Pete at the counter.

"Anyone here like to play some cheap 9 ball?"

I jumped up from where I was sitting and was about to speak up when Pete gave me a stern look and a barely perceptible head movement. I sat back down.

Pete pointed to Lou who was practicing on the table closest to me.

"He may want to play."

I had been watching Lou practice because he played on a professional level. Lou had been a tournament player in his younger days. He was older and didn't play that much but still had a strong game. They started playing 9 ball at five dollars a game. It went back and forth for a while, but after an hour or so, Lou quit. Agusatee tried to talk up another game, but no one would play him after beating Lou. A large crowd watching the game with Lou remained around the table. Agusatee set up a very hard shot and started playing to the crowd.

"Anybody wanna bet I can make this shot."

There were no takers. He tried to make the shot and missed it twice. Then someone bet him a dollar he could not make it in three tries. The dollar was put up on the pool table rail, and Agusatee missed the shot three times in quick succession. Pete looked at me with a smile and nod of his head, as if to say,

"He's got them now."

Agusatee said, "Hell, that shot's impossible, how about this one?"

He lined up another shot to be bet on. Soon the pool table rail was lined with money. If he missed the shot he paid off the row of bills. When he made the shot he scooped up the money. When the bets died down, he would propose a tougher challenge.

"OK, how about if I shoot one-handed."

If there were one or two bets on the rail he might miss the shot and pay the betters. If there were a lot of bets or a big bet, he would make the shot, sometimes on the last try. He was in complete control, regulating the bets by his performance and carnival-like banter. He would bank one rail and two rails; he would shoot the cue ball off the rail. He set up combination shots and jump shots. With each seemingly impossible shot, he would get a few more bets. It got to a point where no one wanted to bet. Finally, he set up a long, extremely hard cut shot from one side of the table to the other.

He was aiming the shot while talking to the crowd. "Come on, who wants to bet I'll make this on the first try?"

He had won a lot of money, and everyone was reluctant to bet.

Still down on the shot, he turned his head to the right, looked me in the eye, and said, "Hey kid, this is for free."

Without looking back, he shot the ball cleanly into the pocket.

After he left I asked Pete, "Hey did you know that guy?"

"Yeah, he came through here a couple of years ago. Did the same thing, cleaned everyone out."

Then there was Otto, a huge man in his sixties with a Russian accent and no teeth. He was friendly, outgoing, and humorous. He had a million stories he would recount to anyone willing to listen. The stories were not funny, but everyone would be laughing because Otto was funny.

The man did not play pool in the conventional sense. He would stand at the end of a table and place an object ball on the foot spot. Then he would take the cue ball in his hand and flick it with a tremendous amount of spin. The ball would travel, hitting three rails. First the long rail to his right, then the short rail opposite him, and finally the long rail to his left and strike the ball he had placed on the spot. He regulated the cue ball's speed by the amount of spin he put on it.

He would do this several times, nudging the object ball until it was deposited into the corner pocket on his right. The accuracy that he was able to achieve was incredible. Like Agusatee, he was personable, engaging, and able to get people to bet on how many turns it would take him to deposit the ball in the pocket. Also like Agusatee, he would lose small bets and win larger bets.

When people would get discouraged because they could not win, Otto would increase the difficulty.

"Ok, I'll put two balls up and make both in the same pocket."

Like Agusatee, it wasn't just his amazing skill, but his ability to negotiate a bet where the victim thought they had the advantage that was key to success. Otto had a skill and an act that he turned into a very profitable business.

After my game with Dan, I was eager to get back to playing competitively. I beat Dan easily, but I'd need a lot of practice to play at my previous level. The pool room we had played in was a dump. I found a nice room a short drive across the Tappan Zee Bridge in Nanuet, New York. It was a strip mall storefront in the center of town. Usually poolrooms were found in the low-rent, high crime areas.

This was a busy shopping area with stores and restaurants within walking distance. There were ten tables in two rows with comfortable seating at each table. The owner greeted me from the counter by the door.

"Would you like a table?"

"Yeah, thanks."

"Take any one you like; the balls are there."

"Ok, thanks, I'll take that first one." I chose the nearest table to the counter. I thought I might engage in idle conversation to explore the current culture in the pool world.

"Oh, you don't want that table; it's Toby's practice table; nobody plays on it."

"Who's Toby? What's wrong with it?"

" Toby was the former owner; he set that up special to practice. Most people can't make a ball on it."

The guy laughed.

"Well, can I take it anyway?" I was curious at this point. Maybe it would be a good practice table for me.

"Sure, go ahead, you can always switch tables."

I chose a house cue from the wall rack and inspected the table. It was an older Brunswick, Gold Crown, in beautiful condition. I could see the outline of the pocket shims installed to make the pockets smaller. Two balls would not fit across the width of the pocket, maybe one and a half. That's what we call a tight pocket table. I struggled to make three or four balls in a row. Every shot had to be deadly accurate and at "pocket speed". At certain angles, no matter how accurate you were, if you hit the shot too hard, the ball would not go in.

"I guess Toby was pretty good." I said.

"I'll say, he came back from a road trip with enough money to buy this pool room."

I made idle chatter with the owner, Phil, explaining I had been away from the game for a while and I needed practice and a new custom cue stick. He had a few two-piece cues behind the counter for sale, but they were of inferior quality. In my hurry to get home, I had left my cue in my locker in San Diego. Phil had a catalog from McDermott Cue Company on the counter. All the way in the back of the catalog was a beautiful two-piece cue with ivory-like inlays in the butt. It was six hundred dollars with an extra shaft, and I asked Phil to order it for me.

"What the hell do you need such an expensive cue for?" he asked.

"Well, I don't know yet, I'll have to see how the practice goes."

A few weeks later I was back at the poolroom.

"Hey, my cue come in?"

"Got it right here," Phil said. It was in a cardboard sleeve wrapped in plastic. I bought a cheap case and told Phill I'd take a table.

"Ya want Toby's practice table again?"

He smiled, mindful of my last visit.

"No thanks, I'll take the one next to it".

It was a fine-looking cue with a glass-like finish. Sixty inches long when put together, it was about twenty ounces with a rock-solid hit. Now, all I had to do was get my game back with a few hours of practice. I was drinking a soda, taking a break, when three men walked in.

There was something odd about the group that caught my eye. The first in the door was an older gentleman, impeccably attired with an air of sophistication. The other two, who were much younger, dressed casually and carried cue cases.

The older man directed one of his companions, who was African American, to a distant chair. He then approached the desk with the other, who was a Tom Cruise lookalike. I strained to pick up bits and pieces of the conversation. They were here looking for a player named George who might play the white guy for some money.

Phil made a phone call, and there was a nodding of heads and, I assume, an agreement of some sort. The white player started practicing on Toby's table. The tight pockets didn't seem to give him any problem. The older gentleman began walking around as if just passing time. He walked over to my table and noticed my new cue on the table.

"Is this yours?"

"Yeah, I just got it."

"It's a beauty; I've seen this one before; it's a McDermott, right?"

"Yes, it is." He sat down alongside me. The chairs were attached, so he was sitting close.

"My name's Larry."

"Fred," I replied.

"Nice to meet you Fred. Do you know this fellow George?"

"No, I'm pretty new around here."

"Yeah, me too. That's Sammy," he continued, pointing to the young man practicing, "and that's Black Dave over there."

I had to chuckle to myself, as I wasn't sure if he was telling me that Dave was black or that the guy's poolroom nickname was "Black Dave". I don't know who White Dave may have been, but I assume you had to be more specific to avoid confusing the two Daves.

Larry was a down to earth, personable character. There were no pretenses with him. He spoke honestly and matter-of-factly. He satisfied my previous curiosity with a full explanation.

"I usually back the Filipinos, but Sammy wanted to play this guy George, so I figured I'd put him in the game."

It was clear now Larry was a stake horse. He backed some of the best pool players in the world in money games. Over the years, I would get to call Larry a friend. Even though he did not play pool, he knew more about the game, including pool rooms and players, than anyone. He could predict the final score in high-level games more often than not. Larry put up money amounting to tens of thousands of dollars in many high-stakes games.

"These guys play out of the West End Pool Room in Elizabeth, New Jersey; have you ever been there?"

"No."

"Ya gotta go, there's plenty of action, good food, and on any given night there are ten, fifteen players that can run a hundred balls, there are tournaments-"

He stopped mid-sentence when the door opened.

George was a skinny kid around 19 or 20 years old. Larry got up to join in conversation with George and Phil. Soon, Sammy and George were in a heated discussion, which was getting louder. Larry shrugged his shoulders and came back over and sat down.

"These kids don't understand; I hate making these games. Young kids always have to argue. Just put up the money and shoot it out. Hell, I'll let them argue it out."

After a few more minutes of discussion, Sammy yelled over to Larry, "Race to five for five hundred."

Larry replied, "No," pausing a moment to think, "make it eight hundred."

George and Phil discussed this proposal and agreed to play 9 ball race to five games for eight hundred dollars. Black Dave sat quietly, seemingly disinterested in the drama. George won the first match and they agreed to play a second match. Larry walked over and handed Phil eight hundred dollars. When he came back and sat down by me he didn't seem concerned and continued our conversation. Both players were good, rarely missing a shot on Toby's tight pocket table. It was close, but I thought Sammy to be the better player. George was good, but he struggled to be good. Sammy was smooth.

Sammy won the second set, and George refused to play him again. I'm not sure what his complaint was.

George pointed at Black Dave, who had been all but forgotten. "I'll play him!"

Dave didn't get up or say a word. George bypassed Phil and negotiated directly with Larry. "I'll play him, eight ahead for a thousand."

Larry balked at this proposal, "eight ahead, we'll be here all night. It'll take too long."

Dave was now out of his chair, screwing his two-piece cue together as he walked over to Larry, "eight ahead is good, I'll be quick."

Larry yelled to Phil, "Alright, eight ahead, but you gotta play for fifteen hundred."

They split the first four games and then they were back to even.

Larry looked at me and smiled. Nodding toward Dave he said,

"Ya gotta be careful what you wish for."

Dave ran five racks without George getting out of his chair. He then got two more to go seven ahead, then won the last rack to go eight ahead when George missed an easy six ball.

Larry said, "I hold Black Dave back just in case."

The brief conversation I had with Larry about the West End Poolroom in Elizabeth piqued my interest. It was a long drive from New York, over the George Washington Bridge and down the Jersey Turnpike to Elizabeth. I walked in the front door, and I was in a game room with stuffed animals hanging from the ceiling. There were coin-operated machines of all types filling the crowded room; the stuffed animals were prizes the younger customers could win. There was a small restaurant on one side, but no pool tables.

"Am I in the wrong place?" I murmured.

I asked an employee if there were pool tables.

"Yeah, they're in the back".

I walked to the rear and found a solid door with a DO NOT ENTER sign. Taking a chance, I opened it and stepped through into another world. I stood on a walkway about ten feet wide running the room's length. The walkway overlooked seven pool tables on each side. A railing with a small shelf separated the walkway from the playing area. Chairs lined each side of the walkway. The room was crowded, and each of the tables was in play. I was trying to take it all in when I heard a familiar voice.

"Hey, Fred, over here." It was Larry. "Sit here."

Larry motioned me to an empty chair.

"Glad you could make it," he said, "but you gotta keep in mind a couple of rules."

"Rules?"

"Yeah, Speedway Stan's the owner and he's a little strange. Only the players are allowed by the tables. Everyone else has to stay up here."

That seemed reasonable to me.

He continued, "If you're watching a game you must be seated."

"Ok," I said.

"Most important, if you wear a baseball cap, which I see you don't, but if you ever do, do not wear it backward."

Larry and I were talking when his attention was diverted.

"Hey Stan," he called, "I want you to meet someone. This is my friend Fred from New York."

Larry introduced me to Speedway Stan, who owned the room and apparently a gas station.

Stan came over somewhat animated, as if happy to meet a new customer. He was maybe forty, balding, and sporting a stocky frame. We exchanged greetings, and before leaving, Stan said,

"Wanna play some cheap 9 ball sometime?"

"Yeah, as long as you describe cheap."

"Twenty-five or fifty, nothing too rich," he said over his shoulder as his attention was diverted to another customer.

After he left, I said to Larry, "Seems like an OK guy."

"Be careful," Larry said, "he's bat-shit crazy."

I was in awe of my surroundings; Ray Martin, a world champion, was in the middle of a 150-ball run on the table right in front of me. Upon winning that game, he played two more games of straight pool each of which he ran 150 balls and out. Jack Colavita played 9 ball on the table to my right with a young hustler. Speedway

Stan put him in the game for five hundred a set. Two seats over from me, Steve Mizerak of TV and beer commercial fame was watching the same games.

Larry said, "There's half a dozen famous world champions in here right now, and a couple of guys you never heard of that could beat all of them for a grand a set." After a pause, he continued, "For the money, I'd put Black Dave up against any of them."

I became a fixture at the West End Pool Room for the next several years. I loved playing pool, but also devoted much time to studying skilled players. I wanted to know what made them so good. I could study, and even play against, world champions and shrewd hustlers in that pool room. My game improved rapidly. I competed in the twice-per-week tournaments held in the upstairs tournament room. Only Jack Colavita had more wins than I did.

One particular night, after winning the tournament and five hundred dollars, I walked out of the poolroom at three in the morning to find my brand new Cadilac had been stolen. Elizabeth, New Jersey, was a cesspool, and The West End pool room was in the worst part of town. There were numerous accounts of players being mugged coming and going. Speedway Stan didn't let any of that enter his pool room. Maybe his weird rules kept the vermin out. On one occasion, a young fellow walked in wearing a baseball cap backward.

Stan said, "Turn your cap around."

"What for?" He ignored Stan and kept walking.

Stan physically attacked the man, throwing him out bodily.

Another time a patron was standing behind the row of chairs watching a game.

"Hey, you have to be seated," Stan said.

The man looked around and replied, "There's no empty seat, Stan."

Stan's reply, "Then get the fuck out!"

The patron quickly found a seat.

I accepted Stan's offer to play some cheap 9 ball. I always played for money but never considered it gambling. I carefully picked my games and rarely lost. When I did lose it was money I had won from someone else. I was never greedy and often allowed players to win when it worked to my advantage. I never played for big money. That requires a different set of skills and nerves of steel.

Ray Martin, for example, was a world champion. He played the best pool I have ever witnessed. Black Dave was not as good as Ray. For a thousand dollars a set Dave would win every time. The money was what made the difference.

One day Stan wanted to play a race to seven for fifty dollars Since he was the poolroom owner, I figured he must be pretty good, but I could afford to lose a couple hundred if it came down to it. It never did.

Larry's haunting words returned to me.

"Be careful, he's bat-shit crazy."

I played Stan quite often over the years. I was a much better player than he was, but he would never accept that.

He chalked my wins up to luck and would curse me vehemently every time we played.

"You lucky son of a bitch." Was among the nicer terms he called me.

He would throw temper tantrums and physically threaten me. On more than one occasion he broke very expensive cue sticks. He would take his cue stick and scramble the balls on the table with it. I considered just not playing him to avoid any confrontation, but he really pissed me off. Besides, I wasn't lucky, I was damn good.

He would win a set or two, but I would win three, four, or more. In most encounters, I would come out ahead two or three hundred dollars. I was steadily winning money from him. In a similar situation I might lose every once in a while on purpose, to keep my opponent engaged. However, in Stan's case I didn't care if he quit. I always played my best game and always walked away with the money. I don't put much importance on the money, but it was the best way to keep score.

"You lucky fuck, I'm a better player than you, why can't I win?" he would say.

"Don't let it bother you, Stan, everybody else has the same problem."

I made many friends at the West End Poolroom and improved my skill and knowledge of the game. I had the opportunity to play some of the best players in the world. Although I had yet to meet him ,I continued to hear stories about Toby. He was described as a thin man with long blonde hair wearing bell bottom pants. He played for large sums of money and seldom, if ever, lost. It was as if he was a myth.

I'd earned a nickname at the West End- I was known as "New York Fred". It was a long drive to the West End from my home in New York, but I considered the distance a positive. I was a rising star in the Department of Correction in New York, and I did not want to run into any former prisoners in the local pool rooms. I had two contradictory lifestyles. No one in the pool room knew I was a Prison Warden by day and likewise no one in the law enforcement community knew I was a pool hustler by night.

It was like I was leading two separate lives, compartmentalized as they were. I even felt like I had two different personalities. One for my professional life and one for the pool rooms. I never considered myself a hustler although that was essentially what I was doing.

Money wasn't the important factor but as I have said it was the best way to keep score.

Playing really good pool was hard work requiring intense concentration. Without the incentive of a sizeable bet on the game I was unable to play at the level that satisfied me. Money didn't motivate me, playing a perfect game did.

One day I took off from work at the Penitentiary to play some pool.

"Captain, come out to my office." I spoke into the phone.

A few minutes later the day shift Captain entered my office.

"What's up Warden?"

"How is everything on the Pen side?"

"Everything's quiet."

"Good, I'm going to take the afternoon."

"No problem boss, I'll handle it."

Captain Rodsky was the best I had. I knew he could handle it.

A professional pool player that I knew casually had quit the drudgery of traveling to tournaments and opened a poolroom in Brewster, New York. It was a 45-minute drive from the prison. I figured I'd check it out and maybe get a game.

I had never played Steve, but we had met once or twice at tournaments. He recognized me as soon as I walked in. It was a nice poolroom, well lit, and in the center of town. After some niceties we decided to play a friendly game of straight pool, one hundred points for fifty dollars. I played a good game of 9 ball but straight pool was my best game. I won a close first game and ran away with the second. Steve wanted to switch to 9 ball where he figured he had a better chance. We played two sets of 9 ball race to seven for a hundred each set. I won both and I was up three hundred dollars when Steve quit. I packed up my cue and as we walked back to the front we passed a billiard table. Billiards was played on a table with no pockets and three balls. You score points by striking three cushions and two of the balls in a particular order.

"Do you play billiards?" Steve asked.

"Not really, I know how to play but just don't normally get the opportunity."

"How about you give me a chance to get even? Play a game of billiards, fifteen points for the three hundred."

I could tell Steve felt he had the advantage here. I was being hustled.

I had only played 3 cushion billiards a few times. Most poolrooms don't even have a billiard table. However, the same principles can be applied from pocket billiards, so I agreed to play. The worst that could happen would be to break even.

I played a decent game and managed to win fifteen to thirteen. Steve had to retrieve my winnings from a cigar box under his front counter. Probably the proceeds from his poolroom last night. He was counting out my three hundred in mostly fives and tens with a few twenties when I noticed a chess board and pieces on the counter.

"You play chess?" he asked.

"Not since I was in the Navy, a friend taught me aboard ship."

I recalled Gary, the shipmate who had taught me how to play during those boring weeks at sea. We played for days on end, twelve sometimes fifteen hours a day. Finally, when I got good enough that Gary could no longer win, he threw the chess set overboard.

"One game for two hundred," Steve suggested. "I'll take white since you're ahead six hundred."

We were about fifteen moves into the game when I sacrificed my queen to trap his king with my rook.

"Checkmate."

It was nice to get out of the Pen for the afternoon, and better to be eight hundred dollars to the good.

The Author, "Floridafred"

Chapter 6

FLU SEASON

While I was making a triumphant return to the pool halls, new positions for Captain and Assistant Warden had been created, and a new training curriculum had been established for Correction Officers. Deputy Sheriffs continued to be peace officers by law but were now officially known as Correction Officers.

A written test was scheduled for qualified officers vying for promotion to captain. A candidate had to be in the top three test scores to be promoted, I was one of three appointed to the position of captain. The department was growing exponentially in all directions. Officers had to be hired and trained to cure the chronic shortages. The prisoner population also continued to grow, causing overcrowded conditions. Temporary structures had to be constructed to house prisoners until permanent buildings were designed and built. Demands to service forty-four local police jurisdictions plus state and federal agencies was straining the new department.

Senior employees had to be designated as instructors to train new employees and even some senior employees who had never received training. The FBI's nearby training facility welcomed local law enforcement to attend alongside FBI agents. I attended a two-week Firearms instructor course. For the first time, Correction Officers would receive firearms training and be required to qualify to carry a firearm. Additionally, I attended the instructor's course for personal combat. I was now certified by the FBI to instruct others in all sorts of violence.

I was establishing myself as a leader. The department was growing so fast that no one could keep up with the increasing demands for staff and space for the expanding prisoner population. I supported the officers who worked for me and backed them in the proper performance of their duties. I made it clear that prisoner abuse would no longer be tolerated. Violence would be a part of the job as long as violent people were admitted to the jail. We had no choice but to win every violent encounter. Therefore, violence would be met with whatever force was necessary. However, once a prisoner was under control, there would be no retaliation or abuse.

I established a relationship with my officers and a reputation among the prisoner population that would get me through many difficult situations. In this business, credibility is your most essential tool. If you lose it or don't establish it, the results could be catastrophic. I barely had time to grow into my new position of captain when I was promoted to Assistant Warden.

Warden, Assistant Warden, Senior Assistant Warden, and Associate Warden were almost interchangeable titles that I held at one time or another. Those titles changed, seemingly at someone's whim, even though the responsibilities remained for the most part the same. I was transferred to the Penitentiary and back to the jail as often as one or the other had problems nobody else could solve.

During one episode, I was the Warden at the Penitentiary. The jail was undergoing a full-scale riot. The jail and Penitentiary were side by side. Prisoners could see windows being broken out at the jail and hear the general chaos as it unfolded. The Penitentiary was an open architecture design in that two hundred or more prisoners ate in the mess hall at the same time and used dayrooms and outdoor recreation freely. Twice a day prisoners had to be locked into their cells for a proper prisoner count.

Because of the jail riot, the Penitentiary prisoners refused to leave the mess hall to be locked in for the count. It was rumored that if they locked in, they would remain locked in until the jail riot was resolved. That was a realistic concern on their part because it would be prudent to lock down the population to keep the jail riot from spreading.

Some penitentiary prisoners sympathetic to the jail riot wanted to start their own insurrection. The jail staff had fled the building, leaving the prisoners to their own devices and facilitating widespread destruction. I was very concerned that the riot could spread to the penitentiary out of sympathy for the jail prisoners, if nothing else.

I entered the mess hall and walked around the group of prisoners who had refused to leave, sizing up the situation. It was dead quiet, and every eye was on me. I stopped at a point where the windows overlooking the jail were to my back. The sound of the destruction going on at the jail permeated the room.

I put one foot on a chair, leaned on my upper leg, glanced about for a minute, and then simply said,

"What's up?"

I held a hand up to the following tumult,

"One at a time."

A spokesman emerged, voicing concern about indefinite lockup. There was a lot of back and forth, complaints, and threats from prisoners. Eventually, I proposed a solution to the two hundred or so present.

I admitted to the prisoners that it would be standard practice to lock down the population for security reasons, considering the problems at the jail. However, if I could count on everyone, to cooperate, I would give my word that I would not lock down the population.

"If we can come to an agreement, the penitentiary will operate normally regardless of what happens next door. Prisoners will be required to lock in for the count as usual, but once the count is completed, the population will be released from cells."

Many inmates protested that I could not be trusted to release them after the count as promised. However, prisoners in leadership roles spoke up.

"If Warden Kenney gives you his word, you can take it to the bank."

This was the credibility I had worked hard to establish. With key prisoner backing, the proposition was met with agreement by the population. Locking down the population would have meant canceling visitation and recreation. I can't blame them for being concerned. The inmate population left the mess hall and locked in for the noon count. I was summoned to the Commissioner's Office upon leaving the mess hall.

Commissioner Allen V. Washburn was a commissioner who wanted to micro-manage everything. He caused many problems and always managed to blame it on someone else. Some conditions that led to the jail riot were due to the Commissioner's management style. Jail management at the time feared him and was tentative in dealing with problems for fear of upsetting him. That let minor problems grow into large ones that could have been dealt with when they were easily managed. Fear of acting on minor issues led to the jail riot and millions of dollars in damage. Instead of supporting his staff, Washburn wanted to keep them fearful and weak, increasing his power.

When I arrived at the Commissioner's office, he held a posture I was familiar with. His swivel chair was turned slightly away from me, and he did not look at me, but gazed out a window.

"Warden, why haven't you locked down your population?" he asked.

"Commissioner, I've just met with the population and received their assurance of cooperation. In return, I promised I would not lock them down."

I could see his jaw grinding away and his face slightly blushed. This was a sign of his anger, or psychosis, that I had previously witnessed.

"Warden, I strongly urge you to lock down your population," he said, then added after a slight pause. "It's your Penitentiary and your decision to make, but it's your career that hangs in the balance."

I doubted he would order me to lock the Penitentiary down because that would give him ownership of resulting repercussions. My career was in the hands of a few hundred criminals.

Without giving me a chance to reply, he said, "That's all, Warden."

Not only did I not lock them down, but I scheduled a special movie night. It wasn't bribery by any means. I wanted to keep them busy and occupy their minds with something other than the jail riot. It was not by accident that the movie had some sexual content. During the entire episode, there were fewer problems than at any time I can recall. The inmate population kept their word and then some.

I was in my office when a delegation of jail officers came to me with an offer. The jail officers had refused to reenter the jail to restore order because they had no trust in the leadership at the jail. However, they would reestablish control of the jail if I would lead them. I went to the commissioner and volunteered my services. I was quickly turned down. If I were to put an end to the jail riot others would suffer professional embarrassment. It came down to politics as usual.

Instead, a tactical unit was called in from the state prison system. It was a terrible idea for several reasons. It was demoralizing to the jail staff. It created a greater danger of severe injuries to the inmate population. The state tactical squad had no ownership concerns for the jail, after the riot was quelled, the jail staff still had to manage the building. The state tactical unit could walk away without concern for future operations or the consequences of their actions.

If I had been allowed to lead a recovery force into the jail, we could have restored order quickly without undue injury or further damage. I had spent years building up my credibility with staff and prisoners. Riots get started and out of control quickly with little or no thought by either side for the consequences. At some point, the rioters, or at least the leadership if it exists, realize they need an endgame. When that happens trust and credibility come into play.

The state tactical force entered the jail and ended the riot by way of brute force. It was, of course, considered a success. After it was over, I entered the jail and went to the booking office which overlooked the recreation yard.

Looking out the window into the yard, I could see several hundred naked inmates standing in rows with helmeted state tactical officers in what I would call a victory celebration. They were shouting at and threatening prisoners into compliance. I heard someone laughing at my side as I watched this sideshow. When I turned toward the laughter, I was surprised to see Commissioner Washburn obviously enjoying the show. I returned to the penitentiary, relieved the riot was over but angry at the abuse tolerated by incompetent officials.

The Department's continued growth afforded Commissioner Washburn the opportunity to appoint a Deputy Commissioner. I wondered if this person was his choice or just another political appointment. His name was Scott Lincoln, a worm of a man with an impressive vocabulary.

Deputy Commissioner Scott Lincoln was unaffectionately called "Scuddy" behind his back. He would have conversations with people who, by their expressions, obviously had no idea what he was saying due to the complexity of his vocabulary. However, he fit right in as Commissioner Washburn's deputy and hatchet man.

During one unusually nasty winter, the flu was prominent among staff and the prisoner population. The list of sick calls to see the doctor was increasing by the day. I began getting numerous complaints and requests from prisoners demanding flu shots be given to the population. I conferred with the medical staff, who determined that flu shots would be inappropriate, but they would see anyone with complaints. The doctor treating penitentiary prisoners reported that he had not seen any severe cases. Still, complaints were increasing to a hysterical level. He felt some symptoms being reported were induced by general fear and were not legitimate.

On one particular day, there was a long line for sick call. A large number of prisoners had collected outside the medical clinic. The doctor examined a record number of prisoners that day, but when it was time for him to leave, the crowd of inmates outside objected so much that he was afraid to leave the clinic.

Inside the locked and secure clinic there was a Correction Officer, a female nurse, and a doctor. The crowd grew to about two hundred prisoners who refused all orders to disperse. I had the bell sounded for a general lock-in with an announcement for all prisoners to lock in their cells. None of the Prisoners responded to the lock in announcement.

Tensions were high, and I sensed we would soon lose control. My first concern was for the staff. I had five Correction Officers on post in various cell blocks. I issued the order for each officer to casually walk past the crowd of prisoners in the main corridor to safety behind the main gate. I instructed them to be sure all cells were left open so that if a prisoner chose to return to his cell, he could.

I did not want a confrontation as we were seriously outnumbered. Prisoners were sitting around the central corridor, waiting to see the doctor. It would take days for him to see two hundred prisoners. I had ten

Correction Officers suited up in riot gear out of sight but available at a moment's notice. I prayed I would not need them as ten against two hundred was poor odds. If the shit hit the fan their job would be to get in quickly, get the nurse and doctor, and get out.

Priority one was the safety of the medical staff. I casually entered the corridor populated with Prisoners and made my way through the crowd. I was no stranger to the group as I walked through the prison every day. I made small talk as I worked my way to the clinic,

"How are you feeling?" "Don't worry we're going to sort this out."

I went into the clinic and announced in a matter-of-fact tone,

"Hey doc, I've got someone I need you and the nurse to see; it'll just take a few minutes."

Then to the Correction Officer, "We'll be right back."

I never lie to prisoners as my credibility is always in the balance. The fact that I was speaking to my staff within earshot of prisoners satisfied my principle. If I took the Correction Officer with me, prisoners would realize the doc wasn't coming back. The clinic was secured by a heavy steel door. I knew the officer would be safe once locked in until we were able to calm the situation and retrieve him. I got the doctor and nurse out safely without incident. It happened so fast the prisoners had no time to process what happened.

Once that was done, Commissioner Washburn had to be briefed on the developments. The Commissioner called Deputy Commissioner Lincoln into his office so I could brief them simultaneously. I let them know that things were tense, and I had concerns that a peaceful solution might be elusive. Commissioner Washburn did his typical posturing of avoiding eye contact and grinding his jaw, thinking of how best to insulate himself from the situation at hand.

"Scott Lincoln will be my point man on this. Warden, you are to notify and gain approval from Deputy Commissioner Lincoln regarding any action you undertake. Do you understand Warden?"

"Yes sir, I will confer with the Deputy Commissioner before taking any action."

"Scott, hang in for a moment. That's all Warden."

"Yes, sir."

The medical staff hypothesized this was a mass hysteria event, a type of hallucination brought about by a reinforcing group anxiety. Attempts made to resolve the situation satisfactorily failed that evening. I did not see any reason to negotiate further, but as a show of good faith, I fed the prisoners sandwiches and drinks in the corridor.

Officers informed me that some prisoners were observed arming themselves by removing batteries from radios. C type batteries, when thrown at officers, can cause serious injuries. The Westchester County Police Department was the investigative agency for the Department of Correction. I called and asked the chief to send a detective to the penitentiary to collect evidence for prosecution if need be.

I intended to prosecute offenders if there was violence or any criminal activity. Dan Smith, a young detective from the County Police, responded to the penitentiary. He was very respectful and seemed eager to help. I briefed him on the situation and told him there was food and coffee in the officer's mess and to make himself comfortable. His role would be to collect evidence and prepare court documents should I charge any prisoner with a crime. The crime of assault on a Correction Officer was my primary concern.

The prisoners were in control of the security portion of the penitentiary, but so far it had remained peaceful. The prisoners, fearing that I would bring a tactical team in that evening, began to barricade the entrance to the corridor.

In consultation with the day shift captain, I put together a plan of action to regain control. It took all night to secure the required equipment and properly prepare staff for what was to come.

Upon arrival of the day shift at seven a.m. I intended to merge the night and day shifts into a tactical unit of about twenty-five officers. They would be in full tactical gear and carry full body shields to protect against thrown objects. There were two ways to get into the corridor where the prisoners were congregated. There was the control center and main gate, which was the standard entry point. The main entrance gate was now barricaded by the prisoners. If a tactical unit were to be deployed, this was where the inmates expected them to enter. However, there was also an auxiliary control center and exit door at the far end of the corridor which was seldom used. It led directly outside of the building.

Everything was in place. At five a.m. I telephoned Deputy Commissioner Lincoln at his home. I advised the Deputy Commissioner that I was prepared to retake the institution by force and briefly outlined my plan, which would be implemented at eight that morning.

He replied, "Warden, I don't know what took you so long to act, but I approve of your plan."

With the Deputy Commissioner's blessing, I had complied with Commissioner Washburns' directive.

At eight a.m. we were ready. The tactical unit was suited up and out of sight. I sent one Correction Officer in a radio car with lights flashing and sirens blaring around to the far end of the building and the auxiliary control center. He entered the darkened Control Center with orders to light it up and suggest this would be the entry point for the Tactical Team.

That control center was always dark, but now it was brightly lit and active. Flashing red lights outside the building gave the impression of a large force. Once inside the control center, the officer was instructed to read an announcement over the PA system.

"All prisoners must return to their cell immediately. Failure to do so will result in force being deployed. If you comply, you will not be harmed. The penitentiary will be returned to normal operation as soon as possible. Your cooperation is required."

He made the announcement repeatedly, while simultaneously the lock-in bell was ringing. The bell was intentionally loud normally. No one could ever say they did not hear it. This was well planned to cause confusion and panic among the barricaded prisoners. The prisoners began to tear down the barricade to relocate it to the other end of the corridor, but the tactical unit instead entered from the main entrance gate, originally barricaded but now accessible. This led to even more confusion as prisoners thought tactical units were coming at them from both ends of the corridor. As the tactical unit entered the main corridor, numerous batteries were thrown at them. A few officers received minor injuries, but the shields protected the majority.

The batteries were the only card the prisoners had. Once they had been expended, they were no match for my tactical unit. Thinking we were coming in from both ends of the corridor, they scattered into the cell blocks, most of them locking in their open cells. Except for a couple small pockets of resistance, we were in control within 30 minutes.

It took another hour to do a final cleanup and get a thorough prisoner count. With all prisoners locked in and accounted for, I assembled the entire Correction Staff in the mess hall. I climbed on top of one of the tables to address them. I congratulated them on a job well-done and thanked them for their efforts and support. I also told them there would be no reprisals against prisoners and that I intended to get the penitentiary back to normal as soon as possible. I also allowed anyone to speak up, who might be critical of the operation. To a man they vocalized support for my actions.

Commissioner Washburn summoned me to his office at nine when he arrived at work. I got there close to eleven as I was a little busy. I was briefing Commissioner Washburn on the events of the past twenty-four hours, but he stopped me when I mentioned my call to Deputy Commissioner Lincoln.

He picked up the phone, "Scott, would you come into my office, please?"

Lincoln came to the door but did not enter the office. He just leaned through the door, smug smile on his face.

"Scott," said Commissioner Washburn, "Warden Kenney tells me he spoke to you at five a.m. this morning and you approved his plan to use force against the prisoner population, which has resulted in injuries to staff and prisoners."

Lincoln placed his hand to his chin, turning his head slightly to the side and scrunching up his face as though thinking hard he said.

"Commissioner, I don't recall that conversation."

Commissioner Washburn said, "Thank you, Scott."

As Lincoln hurriedly left, I started to speak but was abruptly cut off.

"That's all Warden," the Commissioner said.

I returned to my office in disbelief at what had just transpired. I knew Lincoln was a worm, but this was far from what I would have expected, even from him. It was another disturbance from the Department of Correction that would be front page. Everyone was scrambling to get out of the way of the blowback. They were political animals who could care less about prisoners or staff. Rumors spread fast that I would be thrown under the bus. A contingent of Correction Officers came to my office.

"Boss, we're behind you all the way. We had a meeting, if they come at you for this every Correction Officer will walk out."

"Look, I can take care of myself. Just do your jobs and don't do anything stupid. It's all going to work out."

I optimistically cautioned and assured them everything would be okay, but I had doubts.

I was sitting comfortably in my office with my feet on my desk, having gone without sleep for a considerable period. I was trying to figure out how the Commissioner would come at me. Probably say that I engaged in force against the prisoner population without proper authorization and bring me up on charges. It would be my word against Deputy Commissioner Lincoln. Hmm, who might win that exchange?

I returned to reality when I received another visitor, Detective Dan Smith whose presence I had requested from the County Police.

"Hi Warden, bitch of a time, huh."

I replied, "Yeah, sure was, thanks for your help."

I hadn't noticed his contribution and wasn't aware of what help he may have been, but I did appreciate his willingness.

He replied, "No problem, Warden, just wanted to drop off my report."

He dropped a sheaf of papers on my desk and departed. I didn't immediately take notice of his report and went back to reviewing the recent events in my mind. I thought about how I might handle Lincoln's bold-faced lie. I should have recorded the damn call.

Not expecting much, I picked up Detective Dan Smith's report. It was an impressive five typewritten pages. As I read, I was amazed at how comprehensive it was. I did not see the detective as the incident unfolded, but he must have shadowed me all night. As I read, I found phrases like "decisive decision making", "extensive planning", and "perfectly executed". Halfway through the report, one paragraph jumped out at me. It read,

"At five a.m., Warden Kenney called Deputy Commissioner Lincoln in my presence and outlined his plan to use force to regain control of the institution. Deputy Commissioner Lincoln approved Warden Kenney's plan, which was implemented as described on the call".

The report, in its entirety, was a fair representation of the entire episode. It was signed by Detective Dan Smith, and a copy had been sent to his Chief of Police. I made several copies, one in particular for Commissioner Washburn upon which I circled the telephone call to Lincoln in red. I took that copy to the Commissioner's office and slammed it upon his desk, probably with more zeal than necessary. I pointed to the paragraph in red, and, without saying a word, walked out of the office.

I did not hear anything for about two weeks. Then, one day, I was summoned to the Commissioner's office.

Commissioner Washburn and Deputy Commissioner Lincoln smiled and welcomed me with unexpectedly warm greetings and handshakes. Instead of being fired, they presented me with a letter of Commendation with a Gold Star. The added Gold Star is an indication of service under hazardous conditions. I was told by each of them that I did an outstanding job under difficult circumstances in restoring order to the penitentiary. They could not condemn me, so they decided to celebrate me. What better way to squash the forgotten phone call.

Chapter 7

HAUNTING MEMORIES

So many people have played a part in the direction my life has taken and the success I have had. There are those I met along the way who gave me a helping hand, or a push when needed. I will never forget them. And then there are those I can't forget, no matter how hard I try.

The New York State Police brought Tivis Troit Hawkins into the Westchester County Jail on July 18th, 1967. He was charged with murder, attempted murder, robbery, and other lesser charges. These horrific crimes had been committed less than six hours ago.

Hawkins, his wife, and his four children had lived on an estate where he was employed as a caretaker. On the evening of July 17th, a young couple, Joseph, aged 22, and Jannette, aged 18, were parked on a darkened road adjacent to the estate. Hawkins accosted them with a knife and forced them to drive to his residence on the estate in their car. He forced them into the basement of his home and tied them up. Once they were tied up, he sliced Joseph's throat so deep that he severed his windpipe. Thinking Joseph was dead, Hawkins placed him back in the cars luggage compartment and returned to the crime scene. Leaving Joseph in the trunk of the car, Hawkins returned home in his own vehicle, previously left at the abduction site.

Miraculously, Joseph was alive and he broke through the rear seat to escape the car. Although severely injured, he managed to make it to a nearby main road before he passed out. He was discovered by a State Trooper and brought to a hospital. Joseph had seen a red car near the original abduction site and memorized the license plate, assuming the car belonged to the perpetrator.

Before passing out on the road, he removed a card from his wallet that had his blood type on it, knowing if he was found, it would save medical people valuable time. Prior to his six-hour, lifesaving surgery, he wrote down enough information to put State Police on the trail of Hawkins.

Within hours, Hawkins was arrested on the estate. A search of the estate revealed the badly beaten body of Jeannette in a garbage bag. With tears in his eyes, a State Police officer told me her eyes were swollen shut, and she had brutal marks all over her body.

Justice was swift in this case. Hawkins was indicted by a grand jury in August of 1967, and in May of 1968, he was found guilty of all charges and sentenced to life in prison. Joseph testified at the trial, pointing to Hawkins as the guilty party. He was a true hero.

Hawkins resided in my jail for the better part of a year. If ever I have seen pure evil, this was it. If given the opportunity, he would kill again without hesitation or remorse. When I did come face to face with Hawkins, I was as stone-cold serious as he was. He spoke little, but his eyes were constantly darting around, looking for an advantage. When taken out to court, it was obvious that he was measuring his captors. He was continually evaluating security. Who was wearing a gun, who wasn't, and where did he put the handcuff key. How big, how old. I never gave him the chance, but it would have ended badly for him if he tried.

***

On March 24th, 1985, Alex J. Mengel was returning from a hunting trip with three friends. They were returning to Yonkers, New York, from upstate, where Mengel had a hunting cabin or, more like a shed. Westchester County Police Officer Gary Stymiloski was patrolling the Sawmill River Parkway and pulled Mengel's car over for a traffic infraction. Officer Stymiloski searched the car, and found rifles in the trunk. He also determined that the vehicle failed the legal requirements to be on the road. The officer informed Mengel that he was impounding the car. Officer Stymiloski returned to his patrol car and called for backup and a tow truck.

Mengel, who was sitting in his car, announced to his passengers,

"I'm going to kill this fucking cop."

Mengel exited his vehicle and casually walked back to Officer Stymiloski, still sitting in his patrol car. Mengel pulled a 9mm pistol, which had been in his waistband, and, at point blank range, shot the Officer in the head, killing him. The passengers in Mengel's car panicked and drove off, leaving Mengel with the dying officer. Mengel then pushed the officer into the passenger's side and drove off in the patrol car.

The backup car headed south on the Sawmill River Parkway called in that he saw Stymiloskis' patrol car headed north. This prompted a search that eventually led to the discovery of the abandoned patrol car containing the body of Police Officer Gary Stymiloski. At that time, the investigation centered on searching for the vehicle Mengel had been driving with the three other occupants.

Meanwhile, Mengel hid out overnight and the next morning hunted for a subject to carjack. He found that subject in the parking lot of IBM in Armonk, New

York. Beverly Capone was leaving work when she was carjacked and abducted at gunpoint. Mengel returned with Mrs. Capone to his shed and hunting area in upstate New York.

Green County Officers were investigating the burglary of a cabin in the vicinity of where Mengel had been hunting. Inside this cabin they discovered Mrs. Capones' ID card. A short time later, Mrs. Capones' naked, mutilated body was found by a canine search team a half mile away. She had been scalped and stabbed to death.

On February 27th, a thirteen-year-old girl in Syracuse, New York, reported that a man dressed as a woman had tried to abduct her. Mengel had dressed in Mrs. Capone's clothing and was wearing her scalp as a wig. He also wore her lipstick and makeup. On March 2nd Mengel was arrested in Toronto, Canada following a police chase. Mengel exited his vehicle with gun in hand, ready to shoot it out with police but managed to drop the gun accidentally and was taken into custody.

In late March of 1985, Mengel was extradited to the Westchester County Jail, where I first met him. This was very personal for me. The murdered Police Officer had two brothers who were also in law enforcement. One brother, a Correction Officer, worked for me. This was a tragedy beyond words for the Westchester County law enforcement family.

In jail, Mengel was uncommunicative and uncooperative. He was confined in Supermax security. More often than not, he had to be forcefully removed from his cell for court appearances. He fought like an animal when it was necessary to remove him from his cell for court appearances. Quite often resulting in injuries to officers. He was a strong and determined individual who had to be carefully dealt with to avoid severe injury or security risk.

Mengel was scheduled to be arraigned in Green County for the murder of Ms. Capone. Correction Officers were prepared to remove him from his cell forcefully. On this occasion he fully cooperated for the first time and walked out of his cell. I was fearful that this was an opportunity that Mengel had been looking forward to. He would be outside the tight security we had placed him in for a brief period.

Two New York State Police Officers were to transport Mengel in an unmarked car without a cage for prisoner transport. I briefed the officers about Mengel's uncooperative nature and his out of character cooperation that day. I expressed concern they were underestimating the danger involved in his transport. I pointed out that a proper vehicle with a prisoner cage would be more appropriate. The officers assured me they were well aware of Mengel's history and they were prepared to deal with any situation that might arise.

The transporting officers handcuffed and searched Mengel. The handcuffs were secured to a chain wrapped around Mengel's waist and secured with a padlock. I watched as one officer got into the back seat with Mengel. As they drove away, I had a dreadful feeling. I felt the officers were a little too cavalier about their ability to deal with this monster. Not having a secure transport vehicle for this exceptional case was a huge mistake. Mengel arrived safely for his arraignment in Green County on the murder charge, but the trip back would be a different story.

The same two State Police Officers were transporting Mengel after the court appearance. I believe Mengel knew this would be his last chance to escape. His experience at the Jail was in Supermax security, particularly when in transit to court. When he was transported to court from my jail security was professional and tight. He was chained, hand and foot. He was transported in a prisoner van by himself in a secure cage. The prisoner van was always accompanied by a follow car. The two Correction Officers directly in contact with Mengel had hands on him at all times and were unarmed. Two standoff Officers were both armed with handguns and one with a shotgun. Mengel knew he would have no chance to escape under these strict conditions.

Mengel was on his way back to my jail in the back seat of an unmarked police car. Alongside him sat an armed State Police Officer. He was handcuffed to a chain wrapped around his waist and padlocked. They were on the Taconic State Parkway in the outer lane doing 70 miles per hour just minutes from the jail.

Mengel had been waiting for his chance to escape and was running out of time. In a few miles he would be back in the Supermax security of my jail with no chance of escape. With Mengel's mobility severely limited by the handcuffs and chain, he lunged at the armed police officer sitting beside him. He began biting the officer about the face and neck. He had only one focus, to get the officer's gun. The biting was to distract the officer and cause pain, but only as a means to improve his position and access to the officer's weapon. With every move, even though restricted by handcuffs, he was getting closer to the weapon. The officer driving had to decelerate the car quickly in order to help. He managed to pull the vehicle over, and while the car was still rolling draw his own weapon, turn, and fire point blank, striking Mengel in the head. Mengel was killed instantly, even though he had achieved his primary goal. Mengel lay dead in the back seat with the officer's gun in his hand. The officers escaped death by a fraction of a second. The officer in the back seat had to be hospitalized with severe bite wounds. Mengel would not be returning to the Westchester County Jail. Ever.

***

Deputy Sheriff William Fitzgerald was a close friend and colleague. He had been a Deputy Sheriff for twenty years before I was hired. Bill and his lifelong friend, Deputy Sheriff Joe Singer, were in the Sheriff's Department transportation division. These two Deputies were tasked with transporting prisoners to and from the New York State Prison System. The majority of state prisons were hours away by car.

On a fateful Friday, the 13th in 1968, Bill Fitzgerald and Joe Singer were tasked with transporting three prisoners from Auburn State Prison to the jail. Charles Culhane, Gary McGivern, and Robert Bowerman were being returned to jail pending court appearances related to appeals. The three were serving terms of ten to twenty years. McGivern for an armed robbery in which two police officers had been wounded.

In those early days when I joined the Sheriff's Department, there was no training and a cavalier attitude towards security. The three desperate and violent prisoners were sitting in the back seat of Bill Fitzgerald's personally owned car. The car bore no official markings or lights, and no prisoner transport

160

cage. The prisoners were secured in handcuffs attached to a leather belt around the prisoner's waist with a standard belt buckle in the back. Culhane sat on the car's passenger side behind Deputy Sheriff Joe Singer. McGivern sat in the middle, and Bowerman was behind the driver, Deputy Sheriff Fitzgerald.

As the car proceeded south on the New York State Thruway, the prisoners managed to undo the belt buckle that secured the handcuffs to their waists. One of the prisoners asked to make a rest stop. As the car slowed, Culhane used his handcuffs, now free from the belt, to garrot Deputy Singer by the neck. At the same time, McGivern, who was in the middle, reached over the seat to get Joe Singers' gun. Joe Singer fought back desperately to keep from being choked to death and also to prevent his gun from being taken. He lost the battle for his weapon but fought bravely, giving Deputy Sheriff Fitzgerald time to stop the car and draw his own gun.

As the vehicle slowed, Gary McGivern had possession of Deputy Singers' gun. Deputy Sheriff Fitzgerald and Gary McGivern now faced each other at point-blank range, and both fired. Deputy Fitzgerald was fatally wounded in the chest, and McGivern was hit in the arm, causing him to drop his weapon. Now, both guns lay on the front seat, where Deputy Sherrif Joe Singer managed to retrieve them. With a gun in each hand, he emptied the remaining bullets into the back seat. He killed Robert Bowerman, who had been attempting to attack Deputy Fitzgerald, and wounded the other two prisoners. With a gun in each hand and covered in blood, Deputy Singer ran into highway traffic, trying to stop someone for help. It is understandable no one stopped until a state trooper came by.

After recovering from their wounds, Culhane and McGovern went on trial in Kingston, New York, for the murder of a law enforcement officer. I testified at the trial as an expert witness related to the reason and method of transport. Both defendants blamed the entire episode on the dead prisoner, Robert Bowerman. Sometime after the trial, I received a very gracious letter from the district attorney prosecuting the case. The last line of that letter read:

"I thank you for your participation in the trial, which resulted in a guilty verdict and a sentence of death for each defendant."

Closure was expected but would never be achieved. The death row prisoners over time accumulated a cheering squad, including Governor Mario Cuomo, who commuted the death sentences, allowing for their eventual parole and release from prison. Bill Fitzgerald received no such compassion. Joe Singer was seriously injured and could not speak due to damage to his vocal cords. He suffered numerous health issues and the immobilizing symptoms of PTSD until his death. He lost his best friend and suffered from survivor's guilt. William Fitzgerald and Joe Singer had families that were devastated. The Westchester County Sheriff's Department was also devastated, particularly the Jail Division. Bill Fitzgerald had been a close personal friend. His death was one more torment I would add to my recuring nightmares.

Administrators had little understanding of the policies contributing to this tragedy which affected so many. Why was this transport of dangerous prisoners being conducted in a personally owned car with no marking or prisoner transport cage? How easy might loosening the leather belt securing the handcuffs have been? Why was it even necessary to bring these violent, desperate men back to the jail?

As I recall, these questions received little attention nor remedy. However, the incident was a constant reminder as I grew in my career. The security and safety of my officers would always be my first consideration. This often conflicted with policies and politicians I had to deal with.

***

Capitan Beauvais and I started in the Sheriff's Department at about the same time. Like me, he was appointed because of someone he knew that the Sheriff owed a favor to. Because of the politics, there were several incompetent people employed at the jail. Capitan Beauvais was not one of them. Capitan Beauvais was black, bright, ranging toward cunning, but most importantly, he was not a captain. "CAPITAN" was his first name. However, he played it for all it was worth. In those days, he never said,

"I am a Captain in the Sheriff's Department."

He would instead say,

"I am Deputy Sheriff, Capitan Beauvais. Nice to meet you."

People would assume he held a high rank in the Sheriff's Department.

I recall we were both captains when the position of Assistant Warden opened up. Beauvais and I were on a shortlist generated from a test for the position. Beauvais went out of his way to gain favor and speak poorly of me to administrators. He went to the Warden to plead his case and gain racial favor. The warden was African American and Beauvais thought this would play to his advantage. I know that fact because the Warden called me to his office.

"You got a problem with that boy; watch yourself."

"Yes sir, thank you Warden."

In the end, I was the one promoted, but he followed shortly behind me.

Over the years, our initial competitive nature grew into distrust and downright hatred. There came a time when I was Warden at the Penitentiary and Beauvais was Assistant Warden at the jail. As Warden, my office hours were Monday through Friday with a twenty-four-hour on-call status. As an Assistant Warden in the jail, Beauvais had to alternate weekends with other Assistant Wardens. Since it was all one department, an Assistant Warden in the jail would have that same authority and access to the penitentiary.

Beauvais tested that theory one Saturday morning. He was on duty at the jail but appeared at my penitentiary. He advised the shift captain that he was the Assistant Warden on duty and was there to conduct an inspection. He walked through a calm population, asking officers and prisoners about racial tension and the possibility of potential race riots. I received a call at home from the captain on duty informing me that tensions were rising due to Beauvais's visit. I decided to monitor the situation from home, fearing my presence would further inflame tensions.

Monday morning, I was called into the Commissioner's office to be confronted by Beauvais's report that the penitentiary was on the verge of a race riot. He further stated that I had been informed but was doing nothing about it. I assured the Commissioner that any tensions had been caused by Beauvais and not discovered by him. The Commissioner's parting words to me were,

"It's your Penitentiary Warden... for now."

I gathered my staff and raised hell,

"Why was Beauvais allowed into the building?"

The answer, of course, was,

"He's one of our bosses, how could we keep him out?"

I directed my attention to the men at the front desk responsible for allowing entrance to the building.

"I am giving you a direct order, if Beauvais ever tries to enter this building in the future, you are to shoot him. Do you understand?".

The Officer, with a semi-smirk, replied,

"Yes sir, shoot Beauvais."

I called Beauvais to let him know my dissatisfaction with his visit. I told him that I had given orders that he was to be shot the next time he tried to enter my building.

"Seriously, you don't really think they would do that."

I replied, "I don't know, but they generally follow orders."

I did not hear from or see Beauvais for a very long time after that, and tensions in the penitentiary very quickly returned to normal.

My interaction with Capitan Beauvais would take an unexpected turn with unfolding events. Several abortion clinics in Westchester County were the target of demonstrations. Operation Rescue was a continuing campaign against the Dobbs Ferry Abortion Clinic, where hundreds of abortions were conducted annually. A massive protest was planned by factions in the Catholic Church. Demonstrators came from as far away as California and Washington state and over a hundred alleged Priests and Catholic Nuns were arrested for minor crimes and committed to the Department of Correction.

They arrived on buses and refused to cooperate in any way. Half the buses went to the jail and half to the Penitentiary, in order to distribute the workload. Protestors, now prisoners, had to be carried off buses and refused to give names or allow fingerprints to be taken. It was determined by the Law Department that fingerprints had to be obtained by any means necessary as it was a legal requirement. It was left up to the administration at each location how this was to be accomplished. It was a very serious, high-profile conundrum involving Catholic Nuns, Priests, and others in their senior years. Politicians, including the Commissioner of Correction, wanted no part in the decision making. By leaving it open for interpretation they would have scapegoats should it go badly.

I developed a slow, methodical plan with senior-trained staff in three-person teams to force the physical taking of fingerprints. We would not do a complete fingerprint card; frankly, if the prints were unreadable, I didn't care. The main goal was to have no injuries and to barely comply with the law. Assistant Warden Beauvais was assigned to get fingerprints in the jail as he saw fit. I tried to get my plan adopted across the entire department, but that was denied.

Officials were panicked and looking for deniability. The next day, I had barely begun implementing my plan when I was ordered to stop all forced fingerprinting. The jail had started fingerprinting, resulting in several injuries to elderly protestors. There were headlines in all of the local newspapers decrying the injuries to protestors. Cardinal O'Connor held a press conference in support of the protestors and vowing to visit with them in prison. This was a politician's nightmare, which included the Commissioner of Correction and all County Officials.

Cardinal O'Connor was the leader of the Catholic Diocese in New York City, a compelling figure with the support of the press. Cardinal O'Connor first went to the Jail and was denied entry by Assistant Warden Beauvais. He then came to the Penitentiary, where I greeted him at the door and escorted him to where his flock was held. After a lengthy visit and religious ceremony, we went to my office, where he made known some needs of individual protestors. I assured him I would see to those needs personally.

We sat and had a friendly chat about mundane things. We spoke of the stress in our individual positions and the lure of retirement. I spoke of my desire to move to Florida after retirement, and he said,

"I'll come down, and we can go fishing."

"That would be great Father, I look forward to it."

Upon leaving, he held a press conference in front of the Penitentiary where he called me the Devil himself. When I walked him outside at the end of his visit the press took photographs. They appeared on the front page the next day with the caption, "Cardinal O'Connor with the Devil Himself." We shook hands as he left the penitentiary.

Warden Kenney with Cardinal O'Connor

The papers were headlining the incident each day, referring to the brutal way religious protestors were treated and injured at the Department of Correction. My friend and future fishing partner, Cardinal O'Connor, conducted multiple press conferences to support the protestors and demean the Department. Someone had to be thrown under the bus, and it was decided Capitan Beauvais would suffice.

I was in my office when the front desk officer knocked and came into my office.

"Warden, Capitan Beauvais is here to see you sir. Would you like me to show him in or shoot him?"

The smirk lingered. He was the same Officer I had yelled at. I smiled back.

"Show him in."

Beauvais had been served with official charges stating he was entitled to a hearing and could be reprimanded or fired based on the findings. From personal experience, I knew that when the heat is on the higher-ups, they look to divert blame at all cost. Beauvais wanted me to defend him at his upcoming disciplinary hearing.

The charges were bullshit. Beauvais wasn't smart enough to fully protect himself, but he didn't do anything worthy of being fired. I asked Beauvais why he came to me.

"After all of our history, what makes you think I would help you?"

Beauvais carefully considered his words and spoke them slowly.

"Because you are the best at what you do, and you always do the right thing."

I've garnered several awards for exemplary service and have enjoyed the praise of jobs well done, but that statement by Beauvais, coming from him, is the one I would hang on the wall. I told him I would help him, but only because I disliked this political bullshit more than I disliked him.

I got to work immediately. I interviewed and took statements from everybody involved in the jail operation. I also had photographs taken of various jail areas pertinent to my investigation. Beauvais was charged with misconduct and a failure of leadership, resulting in injuries to protestors. Of course, my involvement was noticed by officials, including the Commissioner of Correction. I was called into Commissioner Jackson's office.

"What the hell are you doing?" he asked.

"Sir, I have been asked by Assistant Warden Beauvais to represent him at his upcoming hearing. I am doing my due diligence in that regard."

"You know, Warden, by doing this, you are putting your own career on the line. Why are you doing this"?

Wow, the bullshit keeps getting deeper.

Beauvais's words echoed in my mind, "Because it's the right thing to do, sir."

When these weak political geniuses start throwing heat around, you must throw some back. The Beauvais threat dragged on for months, with his hearing postponed several times. When it was determined to be safe and everything was in the past, the charges were dropped. Beauvais thanked me, but little changed between us.

'The enemy of my enemy is my friend', but that is only during the battle.

***

Dr. Lothringer worked for me as a psychiatrist. He actually worked for Correctional Health Services, a separate entity within the Department of Correction that employed doctors, nurses, and mental health and social worker professionals. They had their own administrators and payroll. I did not approve hiring personnel for Correctional Health, but this never proved to be an issue.

I dealt with many medical professionals during my twenty-five years in Law Enforcement. Dr. Lothringer was far and away the best at what he did. He had an uncanny ability to accurately diagnose a prisoner's mental condition and predict behavior. In many situations, I counted on his advice and eventually considered him a friend. Because of the political nature of the job and the decision-making that, at a minimum, altered lives, I was under considerable stress. I didn't show it and handled it well, but Dr. Lothringer picked up on it.

I was the big dog, but a lot of the little dogs and some of the bigger dogs were constantly second-guessing me. Harvey could see what no one else could and made it his duty to check in with me almost daily. Harvey was in his fifties, but he looked ninety. He was short and skinny but looked smaller because he hunched over when he walked or waddled. He would stop by my office, and I would take a short break to speak with him about a prisoner, sometimes a staff member, or we would chat for a minute or two. I looked forward to his visits and his counsel.

A disgruntled social worker (whom I never liked) one day broke the news to the entire department that Harvey was a convicted abortion doctor and murderer. A book had been written about the crime, and this social worker discovered it in the library. Dr. Mellon, who was head of Correctional Health, knew of Harvey's past and had approved his hiring after he was paroled from prison. There were calls to fire Harvey, but I went to bat for him and managed to retain him.

As a young doctor, Harvey was performing abortions at his home in Queens, New York. A nineteen-year-old girl died during one such abortion. Harvey had diced her up and flushed her down the toilet, causing a significant sewer problem and legal conundrum for himself. Harvey fled to a small country adjacent to France. To boil the book down to a few sentences, Harvey was extradited, pled guilty to manslaughter, and served more than 2 years in state prison. Notably, at his trial, during which he pled guilty, numerous citizens appeared on his behalf.

This terrible crime destroyed a family, but the man I knew as Dr. Lothringer bore no resemblance to the Queens, New York Doctor in the book. There were calls to fire him, most vocally, from the disgruntled social worker. Officials, afraid of anything that may tarnish them, pressured me to act. But Harvey was an asset to the Department, and I took a lot of heat fighting for him. To my surprise, the entire staff followed my example and went to bat for Harvey, except of course the disgruntled social worker. It was tough for a while, but Harvey weathered the storm and continued serving the Department.

***

The "French Connection" case is one of the most famous drug trafficking cases in American history. It involved a sophisticated scheme to import heroin from Turkey to France and then to New York City in the 1960s and early 1970s. This case exposed an international narcotic smuggling operation and led to significant drug seizures and arrests. It was dramatically depicted in the 1972 film "The French Connection", which further cemented its place in popular culture.

The drug smuggling operation was named after its primary route. It began in Turkey, where raw opium was processed into heroin. It then went to France, specifically Marseille, where the Corsican mafia was involved in refining the drug. From France, the heroin was then smuggled into the United States, particularly New York City, where it was distributed on the streets. This heroin trafficking operation was responsible for a significant portion of the heroin entering the United States during that period.

The investigation into the French Connection was a complex, multi-agency effort that included the New York City Police Department. Detectives Eddie Egan and Sonny Grosso were specifically credited with exposing the largest drug smuggling operation in history. Other law enforcement entities in both the United States and abroad were involved.

One of the pivotal moments of the investigation was the seizure of approximately 112 pounds of pure heroin hidden in a car shipped from France to New York. It was at the time, the largest drug seizure in U.S. history. The street value of the seized heroin was estimated at around $32 million, highlighting the massive scale of the smuggling operation.

The successful dismantling of the French Connection network over a decades long investigation led to numerous arrests and convictions, significantly disrupting the heroin trade routes between Europe and the United States.

A central figure in the case was Jean Jehan, also known as "Frog One", who was a top target in the investigation. He earned the nickname from his status as a key operative in the smuggling operation and his French nationality. Jehan was deeply involved in organizing the transportation of heroin, making him a crucial link between the Turkish suppliers, the French processors, and the American distributors. He was known by several names increasing the difficulty to track his movements.

Little is known about his personal background, the legal proceedings against him, and his ultimate fate. The historical record of Jean Jehan is mostly absent. Other co-conspirators were imprisoned, or murdered, in the United States and France. As arrests were being made by law enforcement, witnesses were being eliminated by the conspirators. References to Jean Jehan all but disappear.

The French Connection film starring Gene Hackman was a fictionalized depiction of the real-life events. In the final scene of the film, Detective Popeye Doyle, played by Gene Hackman, pursues "Frog One", the main conspirator, into an abandoned factory while a shootout between mobsters and police ensues. While Popeye Doyle and Frog One are off camera you hear a single gunshot, and the film ends. Was Frog One shot, captured, or did he escape? It seems in the movie and in real life, no one knows for sure.

So, what did happen to Frog One?

In the early 1970's I received information that. Federal authorities would be arriving with a special material witness. He was to be housed in a special wing with no contact with any other prisoners. The civil section of the jail was a housing unit for this specific task. The cells were more like rooms, providing more space and amenities. Detainees in the area need not come into contact with their neighbors. Federal material witnesses were fairly common at the time. Because of the secluded nature of this living space, federal authorities took advantage of the secure housing. The Sheriff was happy to oblige since the Federal Agencies paid well to keep their important witnesses safe and secure.

French Connection witnesses were being murdered at an alarming rate, making secrecy and safety all the more important.

A man identified as Jocques Bousquet was delivered to the jail by Federal Authorities as planned. He was described as extremely high profile and at great risk of being assassinated if found. It was understood that Federal witnesses were never booked at the jail under their real name. The whole purpose was to keep them off the radar.

He spoke only French with minimal understanding of English. At first, he was very timid and soft spoken in his limited English. Over the next two years I would get to know him quite well. He was a man in his fifties with salt and pepper hair and a goatee. He was of an average build but would exercise in his cell vigorously every day. As he became more comfortable in his surroundings his English improved quickly.

I passed his cell quite often while making my rounds. It was much larger than a normal cell with a full-size bed. Instead of bars, the entire front of the cell was a heavy mesh screen, giving full visibility without the jailhouse flavor.

Early in his incarceration, Federal Authorities asked if he could have a typewriter in his cell. I saw no problem with this, particularly if it was going to be helpful to law enforcement. He never received visitors, but agents would take him out quite often, returning him after several hours. Most of his trips out of the jail were to give testimony on his vast knowledge of the illegal activities related to his case. He had agreed to full disclosure in an arrangement with a federal prosecutor.

Whenever I passed his cell he would stop typing and step to the front of the cell.

"Good morning, Warden," he would say.

"Good morning, Jocques, how are you doing today?"

"Everything is fine sir, thank you."

He never complained or requested anything. He was obviously an intelligent man of some refinement. He could type faster than my secretary.

The day came for Jocques to be taken out for the last time. He asked to see me privately. All the typing for the better part of two years was neither a confession nor information for Federal Prosecutors. He had written a book which had been published. He presented me with a signed copy of his book and he thanked me for my hospitality.

After Jocques left for the last time, I opened the cover to see his handwritten note.

"To Warden Kenney,

With great affection

Jocques Bousquet"

Of course, Jocques Bousquet was his nom de plume. His real name was in fact Jean Johan, "Frog One."

He was responsible for the arrest and conviction of dozens of conspirators in several countries. The arrests and trials of numerous mobsters initiated a murder spree of co-conspirators and potential witnesses.

As he was leaving I asked,

"Are you going to be OK?"

"Yes Warden, everything is good."

The only information I have been able to find on Jean is that he passed away peacefully in his home country of France at the age of sixty-seven. The book he presented me with is written in French and I have no idea what it is about.

Chapter 8

PRIVATE INVESTIGATION

A Correction Department colleague and I were discussing the possibility of starting a security business as a sideline. It would necessitate being licensed as private investigators, among other business requirements, but we were just testing the waters and doing research.

I assumed I had the necessary experience required to apply for a Private Investigators license. I filed my application and waited for a reply. Two investigators from the Department of State showed up at the penitentiary to question me about my application. They requested to see every investigation I had ever conducted. My secretary recovered dozens of cases in which I was the prime investigator, going back to when I was a Captain. The investigators spent the entire afternoon going over every case and making notes.

Meanwhile, I wanted to experience the work and get some idea of how the management of such a business operated. I applied to the Pinkerton Detective Agency for a part time job and was referred to a fellow named Tony, who was in charge of a special investigative division.

The primary business of Pinkerton Detective Agency was supplying both armed and unarmed uniformed guards to various companies. I was not looking for a steady job but something I could do occasionally as my time might permit. Considering my position as Assistant Warden, I had to choose supplemental work carefully so there would be no conflict.

Tony had just the deal for me. He would call when he had the right job, and if it fit my needs, all well and good. Tony handled cases requiring a great deal of specialized skill , so he was willing to accommodate me. Pinkerton did not advertise this type of work. It was mostly word of mouth or referrals from their uniform division. Tony advised me he had another special operator, whose name was Sal.

"You will get to meet him; you have a lot in common."

It was only a short time before Tony called to offer me an assignment.

The client was a well-known fast-food franchise that contracted with Pinkerton to provide detailed information on various stores in their franchise. My assignment was to visit a list of stores located near New Jersey Turnpike exits. Twice a week I would drive down the Jersey Turnpike, visiting stores along the way. It didn't matter when I went, so I could work it into my schedule.

The client requested a detailed report regarding cleanliness, conduct of staff, and any other information I deemed pertinent. Sliced deli meat, cigarettes, and other random items were purchased at each location. I would submit receipts with my report for reimbursement. While I was required to turn in any purchased cigarettes, I had discretion over the disposition of the other items. On most nights, I would bring home twenty to thirty pounds of cold cuts, which I would distribute to friends and family.

Tony told me that the client was impressed with the first reports I turned in. They couldn't say happy because the stores were a mess, and the parent company was losing thousands of dollars to the many scams I uncovered. It takes a trained eye to spot persons trying to look normal while doing clandestine activities, but that had become second nature for me. Cleanliness and staff misbehaving were common and somewhat subjective. Most scams I observed was the selling of items not in the store inventory. Those transactions happened mainly in the evening when management was not present. The later the hour, the more dishonesty occurred.

Employees brought in items to sell and pocket the money. They also used their own bank for these sales, so actual store money was not comingled. Many had their own private store selling cigarettes, sometimes non-taxed, cold cuts, drinks, and other items outside of inventory. They would even bring cups and wrapping papers so the business would not be depleted of those items. One of the ways that the franchise company keeps score is by monitoring the use of bags and cups with the company logo.

The parent company can estimate sales by the amount of paper products used. The bad guys brought cups, bags, and paper to wrap cold cuts that did not have the company logo. I observed the same people hanging around stores late at night making purchases for which they were not charged. I continued the assignment for about three months while the franchise company significantly changed its relationship with the stores.

Tony was so impressed with my work that my next assignment came quickly. The "Crow's Nest" in Nanuet, New York, was a house converted into a bar and nightspot. The owner lived in Florida and had a local manager. The absentee owner was losing money and hired Pinkerton to investigate. Tony assigned one of the Pinkerton secretaries to go with me, thinking a couple would arouse less suspicion.

A PAIL OF BEER

On a Friday night, I picked up Judy and drove over the Tapan Zee bridge to Nanuet, New York. We arrived at the "Crow's Nest" at about 9 PM. It was a two-story residence converted for commercial purposes with a large neon sign displaying a bird in a nest and the words "Crow's Nest" in blue and pink taking up the entire second-floor front. There was a huge dirt parking lot on three sides of the building, and it was full of cars.

We paid ten dollars each cover charge to enter the crowded venue. The first thing I noticed was how large and open the first floor was. It did not appear the second floor was in use, except possibly for office space or storage. A bar wrapped around two sides of the room with barstools accommodating thirty to forty patrons. Another row of customers stood behind the stools. It was a popular meeting place for young adults and others who were not so young.

After a short time, we found two stools at the overcrowded bar. Pizza boxes from an outside vendor were piled high on one end of the bar. Slices were heated in a microwave and sold at a fast clip. One worker alone was working the pizza sales and staying busy. In another area behind the bar cartons of cigarettes were on display. Drinks were expensive, and I could see that some of the alcohol was poured from pint bottles. That made no sense from a business standpoint, and I suspected the bottles were refilled from personal stock.

Upon entering, I noticed that the employee collecting the cover charge used a cigar box to hold the money collected with no visible accountability. Money could be easily skimmed, and I noted that a more accountable system was needed. I could not identify anyone in charge, but each worker remained in position without aid or direction. This place had to be a gold mine for someone, but the question was who.

I typed up a comprehensive report for Tony and dropped it off a day later. Tony called the client in Florida, giving him the highlights before sending my report. A day later, Tony called me and asked if I could come by the office, as the client wanted to speak with me by telephone.

We did a speakerphone conference with Tony and me on one end and the bar owner with his lawyer and accountant on the other. The owner was noticeably upset, his voice shaking on speaker. He expressed his disappointed with management. Apparently it was a family member.

He informed us that he was unaware of a cover charge or the sale of pizza and cigarettes other than a cigarette machine that did not seem to do that well. The owner asked what I thought he should do. His question to me said a lot about him and the situation he found himself in. Victimized as he was, he had no sense of what needed to be done, so I told him.

"Shut it down and start over; there is nothing salvageable."

A week later, the Crow's Nest was closed.

Tony and I became good friends. He would often call me asking for advice on specific jobs he had secured. I was learning some of the basics of managing a security firm. Even though Tony's area of expertise was the investigation side for Pinkerton, he maintained that the big money was in uniformed guards. He gave me all the work I could handle, which had its limits due to my responsibilities as Warden.

Another time I was asked to investigate a well-known hotel bar in Elmsford, New York, just a short distance from home. Management had a suspicion that the bartender manager was skimming money from the register. My investigation revealed he was not only stealing money and giving away free drinks to entice more significant tips, but also running a prostitution business in conjunction with the hotel desk manager!

Rooms on the first floor adjacent to the bar were reserved for prostitution. The girls sat in a booth, posing as customers. Deals were made at the bar. The bartender would call a girl over, and an introduction would be made. The girl would walk alone down a corridor toward the room, followed a minute later by the "John". This was a relatively quiet bar, and it was difficult for me to remain incognito. I figured, eventually, they would make me out to be a cop.

At one point, I was walking close behind a John, hoping to see what room he entered. As I rounded a corner, the girl walked back toward me. I could tell by the expression on her face that I was made. If they thought I was a cop, I was probably safe from violence. However, they might be inclined to explore my motivation to protect their investment. This was no small operation. I suspected organized crime to be involved. I was armed, but discretion is the better part of valor. I had enough for a comprehensive report, so a hasty retreat was the best course of action.

Tony called to offer me a VIP Protection assignment. I had attended classes at one time with the New York City Police Unit responsible for VIP protection. Pinkerton and Tony had secured a job providing twenty-four-hour security for a high-profile individual and his family. The man, Jose Torrillo, owned a vast lumber mill and plantation in South America. He reportedly had union problems that had turned violent. His South American Superintendent had been shot and wounded twice, but fortunately had recovered from both injuries. Jose himself had been attacked outside his home in New Jersey by men with baseball bats. The attack required an extended hospital stay and almost cost him his life.

Tony wanted me to pull a shift in New Jersey at his home, evaluate the security situation, and make recommendations. Jose insisted that all agents so assigned must be armed for his protection. At the time, there was a strange situation between New York City Police Officers who lived in New Jersey, and the New Jersey State and local police. Some New York City Police Officers returning to New Jersey after work were arrested for carrying a firearm. This stemmed from a New Jersey Police Officer detained in New York City on a similar charge. It seemed this was a tit-for-tat feud between law enforcement elements. I was not going to push my luck by getting caught up in the middle of that situation.

I told Tony I could not carry a firearm in New Jersey.

Tony said, "Look, Fred, just tell him you have a gun. You don't really have to carry one."

"Yeah, OK, Tony, and what do I tell the guy that comes after Jose and tries to kill both of us? No thanks."

Jose eventually moved into a hotel in New York to keep the danger away from his family. Tony asked if I could pull an occasional overnighter on a weekend bodyguarding Jose at the hotel. I told Tony I would consider it but wanted more information before committing.

Tony said, "No problem, I'll have Sal call you."

I had not met Sal but knew he was Tony's full-time go-to guy. Sal had been babysitting Jose, even pulling double shifts for weeks. According to Tony, Sal was an ex-cop and really good at what he did. I have a high regard for retired cops, but ex-cops make me wonder just why they are ex-cops. Since Tony spoke so highly of Sal, I decided to give him the benefit of the doubt.

Sal called and filled me in on the client. He didn't think the client was involved in anything illegal and that the union problems in South America may have spilled over to this country. I asked Sal how he dressed and what equipment he carried.

"He likes to dine out so dress for nice restaurants."

"No problem."

"I carry one sidearm and a small overnight bag containing a short-barrel shotgun."

"Do you think the shotgun is necessary?"

"No, it's not, but it impresses the client, being a little dramatic is good for business."

Upon Tony's request I agreed to, a Saturday overnight with the client.

Jose Torrillo was a likable, regular guy, if not a little on the meek side. The hotel room consisted of a bedroom for the client and a living room with a small kitchen, sofa, and TV. It was a relatively comfortable setup. The client said he would like to go out to dinner at about seven. I decided to be a little theatrical since business was what I was here to learn. While we got acquainted, I removed my sports jacket to reveal the 1911 style 45 on my right hip and the two extra magazines on my left side. I wanted to impress the client and let him know he was well protected. As suggested by Sal, I also had a short-barreled shotgun in my overnight bag. I placed the bag on the counter with a clunk. The client could guess what was in the bag, which I slung over my shoulder when we went out.

I told Jose to relax and enjoy his dinner, as he was in safe hands. I cautioned him, however, to do everything I say, even if it seems strange. If I move, you move and stay close. It felt like I was playing a game, but in reality, I had no idea what danger Jose and, therefore both of us, may encounter.

We went to an upscale Peruvian restaurant where I passed the maître de twenty dollars to get a table where I could see the entrance with my back to a wall. Since I was unfamiliar with the food, Jose helped me order, and we had a lovely meal while he told me about his family and South American plantation.

I mentioned that I wanted to build a large deck on the rear of my home and was wondering what type of wood I should use. Jose said he would supply the wood if I gave him the exact dimensions of the lumber I needed or if I had a set of plans he could work from. He explained that the trees on his plantation were impervious to the elements.

"I'll custom cut the wood, put it into a container, and have it shipped to you, no charge. It'll only take a couple of weeks."

I was impressed by his generosity and tempted but felt it would be unethical, so I declined his offer.

We returned to the hotel, where Jose retired to his bedroom. Before doing so, he reminded me that the sofa, TV, and kitchen were for my comfort. His bedroom contained his own TV and a desk where I could see he had been conducting business. I kept the TV on low because I could hear Jose talking on the telephone late into the night.

Watching TV and intermittently dozing off, I was suddenly awakened by the rattle of the chain on the hotel room door. I jumped up to see Jose removing the chain on the inside of the door. It was 3 am as I grabbed my shotgun and pushed Jose away from the door.

"What are you doing?" I asked.

"Someone was knocking on the door," Jose said.

"Jeez," I said, "there's never a good reason to answer the door at 3 am."

I ushered Jose into his room and told him to close the door. There were no more sounds from the hall, if there ever were any. With Jose back in his room, I stayed alert with my shotgun on my lap for the rest of the night.

Pinkerton moved Jose the next day out of an abundance of caution. I pulled a couple more uneventful shifts guarding Jose and struck up a friendship with him. Jose told me he was dropping Pinkerton because some of his employees from South America were coming here to provide security for him.

Jose asked me if I could do one last favor and help him buy a shotgun for personal protection and a bulletproof vest for his sawmill superintendent in South America. I introduced Jose to a friend who ran a Police Supply store to accomplish his request. Jose bought a nice 870 Remington twelve gauge and a bulletproof vest that had SHERIFF in 4-inch letters front and back. It gave me a chuckle to envision his plantation superintendent in the jungles of Peru with his "SHERIFF" labeled vest.

My next assignment from Tony was another overnighter with a twist. The Norelco Corporation had a massive warehouse in the South Bronx and were preparing to release a new coffee maker in time for Christmas sales. According to Tony, everyone in the South Bronx already had one. This vast warehouse encompassed an entire city block and it was hemorrhaging coffee makers. They had been unable to identify or stop the thefts. On this job, I would finally meet and work with Sal.

Sal called to brief me on the job. The plant manager would sneak us in the warehouse's back door after dark. We would remain locked in the warehouse overnight, setting up surveillance in hopes of catching the thieves. Uniformed security guards employed by Norelco patrolled the warehouse at night. They would not be aware of our presence since they had not been ruled out as responsible for the thefts. There were only two unarmed guards. The warehouse was so large that avoiding them should not pose a problem. The plant manager was the only person who would know we were in the building.

Sal asked if I could pick him up since his car was in the shop.

"No problem, be happy to, what type of equipment are you bringing?"

"Two handguns, one on my hip, the other in an ankle holster, and a shotgun," Sal said. "Some tough people may be involved in this."

"OK," I said, "I'll come heavy."

"What are you wearing?"

Sal replied, "Just jeans and a vest."

"Oh," I said, "is it going to be cold?"

"No," He said, "Bulletproof."

On the way to get Sal, I stopped at the jail to pick up my bullet proof vest. As I exited, one of the officers on duty asked with a smile.

"Expecting a tough night, Warden?"

I replied, "Yeah, you never know."

We got off the highway in the South Bronx, the home of the 41st precinct, Fort Apache, a crime-ridden area and the subject of books and movies. It was dark, and the streets were empty; I slowed as I pulled up to a red traffic light. Suddenly Sal yelled,

"What the fuck are you doing, don't stop, go through it, go, go!"

I hesitated, but there was no traffic, so I went through the light.

"What's that all about?" I said to Sal.

He replied, "This is the South Bronx, nobody stops for red lights. If you do, they come out of the sewers and kill you."

We pulled onto a side street behind the huge warehouse and waited. Soon, one of several loading dock doors opened up.

Sal said, "There he is, pull in."

I pulled the car inside the building, and the door closed behind us. The warehouse manager briefed us. We would be locked in until morning when he returned. Except for two security guards, no one else was authorized to be in the building. If we encountered anyone else, we were to consider them trespassing. Security guards make rounds through the warehouse once an hour on the hour, and we should avoid them. They are not armed and should not be a problem.

The warehouse interior was at least 4 stories high, with boxes piled up almost to the ceiling. The floor was at least the size of a soccer field. Pallets of wire-strapped merchandise were in steel racks that reached 30 feet into the air. We selected one such rack overlooking a central aisle with a line of site to the entrance the security guards would enter through. We climbed to the top of the rack and arranged boxes like a fort. Looking high above us, skylights were connected by catwalks all over the ceiling. There was no telling if other ways into the building existed.

We settled in for a long night. Sal casually mentioned that if we apprehended some bad guys, he would most likely fire a couple warning shots into the ceiling from his shotgun.

"Good to know," I said.

We had been watchful for about an hour or so when the entrance door opened, and three men entered. We knew only two uniformed security guards were in the building, so these guys were hostile. We were getting ready to descend on them when it became apparent that each man was carrying a shotgun that had been hidden under the long coats they wore. We watched the three spread out across the central aisle in an obvious search pattern. Then, it became apparent who they were.

We could see the New York City Police shield that hung around each man's neck. They were part of an NYPD Quick Response Anti-Crime Unit that was mobile and responded to violent crimes in progress.

I said, "Sal, maybe we better identify ourselves and let them know we're here."

Sal replied. "Are you crazy? They'll just start shooting; that's an anti-crime unit, they're bad mother fuckers."

We remained hidden, and I was concerned that my breathing was loud enough for them to hear. They swept the entire floor before giving up and leaving. We stayed put for the rest of the night, fearing they would return. The warehouse manager told us the following day that a citizen had observed us entering the warehouse the night before and had notified the police.

I began to wind down my work with Pinkerton as I found myself busy with my investigations at the Department of Correction. A prisoner being held in solitary confinement for assaulting a Correction Officer claimed he had been beaten by three Correction Officers who entered his cell late at night. The Correction Officers maintained that they responded to the cell upon hearing a commotion and restrained the prisoner from harming himself. The prisoner had facial contusions and two giant bruises on his back. The prisoner claimed that the officers attacked him for no apparent reason, kicking and stomping him.

The officers' statements did not match the facts as I saw them. How did the prisoner get the large bruises on his back? To answer this question, I enlisted the aid of the County Medical Examiner. The County Medical Examiner at first thought I was showing him photographs of a dead body. Once I cleared that up, he provided some enlightening information.

One bruise, according to the medical examiner, appeared to be the imprint of a size 12 boot with a distinctive tread. The other bruise was not as clear, but it was likely the same boot. He gave me an official written report and stated that he was prepared to testify in court. When I confronted the officers, they had no explanation for how the bruises occurred on the prisoner's back. One officer wore size 12 boots, which I impounded on the spot. The medical examiner compared the boot to the bruise. In his professional opinion, that boot compared favorably to the bruise on the prisoner's back. He was prepared to state in court that the boot caused the bruise.

I called the County Police and presented them with my evidence. The County Police are the investigative agency for the Department of Correction. One week later, the three Correction Officers were arrested for assault and released on bond. They were suspended from duty pending the outcome of court proceedings.

I was taking a lot of heat for my investigation and the subsequent arrest of the officers. At the time, the officers' union was in negotiation with the County over wages and working conditions. Elections were imminent, and politicians were eager to resolve any issues. My superiors would have liked for this incident to go away.

The prisoner in question was no doubt a dirtbag and may have deserved what he got. It would have been easy for me to agree with that. The problem for me, however, was that this was not a close call. If an officer is attacked and that officer unloads on the prisoner, I will give that officer some leeway. This, on the other hand, was a premeditated attack by three officers who had no business even being in that cell block.

It would be a disservice to every officer if I allowed anyone to think they could get away with this barbaric act. The discipline of my staff would hardly be improved once word got around that I allowed unprovoked assaults to go unpunished. I stood up to the pressure to make this disappear and insisted on prosecution. The powers that be, however, got their way, and the case was initially knocked down to a misdemeanor assault.

Finally, it was referred back to the Department of Correction to be handled as an internal disciplinary action. In the end, the officers received periods of suspension. I was not happy with the interference by county officials, but I had made my point and could chalk up a small victory.

Lock-in at the jail was nine PM, at which time each prisoner would be required to lock in their assigned cell. Up until nine, most prisoners would be in a dayroom adjacent to their cell block watching TV. I occasionally entertained a late lock in request from individual cell blocks to watch a special program. In deciding to approve or disapprove the request, I had specific criteria. What is unique about this program? What has been the level of cleanliness and cooperation of this group as a whole? Why do I want to approve this request? Just making the request was not a reason to support approval. There were security and other administrative reasons to deny all such requests.

I received a written request from the minor cell block on a Friday. These were prisoners from sixteen to twenty years of age, a troublesome group at best. The dayroom was on the first floor and could be observed from the central corridor. A bank of jalousie windows hinged at the bottom ran the length of the dayroom and separated it from the central corridor. Before the construction of the dayrooms, these had actually been outside windows, so there were also bars on the dayroom side of the windows.

I denied the request and signed it to be returned to the prisoners by the evening shift captain. The captain knew the request had been denied, and the prisoners had my signed denial. At nine thirty that evening, I received a call at home from the shift captain. Prisoners in the minor block were refusing to lock in or leave the dayroom. They insisted they be allowed to stay up late, even though the Warden had denied their request. The captain also stated that they had barricaded the dayroom door with furniture.

I directed the captain to prepare a tactical team, line them up in the corridor outside the dayroom and await my arrival. Suiting up a tactical team involved officers with helmets, face shields, body protection, and riot batons. The batons are made of a hefty oak-type wood about two inches in diameter and thirty inches long. This was mainly for show but if I needed them, they would be ready.

Upon my arrival thirty minutes later, I found officers in riot gear standing by in the corridor. The inmates had removed their shirts and fashioned them into headgear with masks. One inmate, evidently the ringleader, was standing at a partially opened window, ready to confront me.

I walked up to the window to speak with the prisoner, at which point he shoved a paper out the window stating,

"These are our demands, Warden."

He then slammed the window shut. He displayed a big shit-eating grin, and the other prisoners were loudly demonstrating their approval.

I pivoted my upper body to the right addressing an officer standing behind me.

"Let me have that baton."

Without waiting for a reply or movement, I snatched the baton from his hands. Then, turning powerfully to my left, I struck the recently closed window as hard as I could with the baton. My effort had the desired effect. The thick tempered glass window shattered into a million marble-sized pieces that bounced around like shrapnel.

Tempered glass does not break with sharp edges like window glass, so although harmless, the psychological effect was still immediate.

There were a number of vocal reactions from inside and outside the dayroom.

"Holy shit!"

"What the fuck!"

Then quiet with everyone seemingly frozen in place waiting for my next action.

I calmly balled up the list of demands and threw them through broken window into the dayroom.

I quietly said to the group, "I'm going to get a cup of coffee; if you're still in this dayroom when I return, I'm throwing tear gas through this window."

"Captain, let's get a cup," I said as I left for the officer's coffee mess.

The captain and I were having our coffee and a pleasant chat when the sergeant came in about a half hour later. The captain asked,

"What's going on out there?".

The sergeant said, "Sir, they're fighting to see who can get out of the dayroom the fastest. We're taking them out two at a time and locking them in."

I said, "Thank you, sergeant, let us know when all is secure."

"Yes sir, Warden."

When all the prisoners were locked in their cells, I went into the cell block and slowly walked past each cell. I wanted to be sure each one saw me and had an opportunity to speak to me if desired. Nobody said a word.

Riot troops, batons, and smashed windows all designed to quell a volatile situation without violence. The end result is a simple message:

"Don't mess with Warden Kenney."

Chapter 9

RETIREMENT

Retirement from the Department of Correction was drawing near, and I could tell I was burned out. Not being one to go along with the make-no-waves flow of things, it seemed I was always fighting the system. I had done everything on my terms and survived, which was remarkable. I was winding down my career and had nothing left to prove. Well... there was one thing.

When I started with the Sheriff's Department, there was no training, not even for firearms. You were either issued a gun or, in most cases, just went out and bought your own and learned how to use it. I was one of the first deputies to be sent to FBI firearms training. Eventually, I went through the FBI Firearms Instructors School. With that foundation, I helped develop training and firearms qualifications. For the past fifteen years, officers have been required to qualify with a firearm once a year.

As one of the department's first firearms instructors, I helped develop firearms training and competency tests.

The process is a realistic test of an officer's safe handling and proficiency with a firearm. The test requires each officer to fire one hundred rounds at various distances once per year. There are slow fire, timed fire, draw and fire and reload events. Every round in the bullseye is counted as one point, and 75 points are required to qualify. Only those qualified may carry a sidearm.

I have qualified with a score of 100 points every year for the last 15 years. Our range officer told me he would happily qualify me based on previous scores, but I would not have it. Several friends showed up at the firing range on my last firearm qualification to cheer me on

Some people were just happy to see me go, but the ones that showed up were indeed the ones that mattered. I fired a perfect score of 100 on that last qualification for the sixteenth year in a row. That is a record that will stand for a long time. With that, I could retire, leaving on my terms with my record in the books.

So many times during the past twenty five years I had been in danger of being forced to leave on someone else's terms. How would I have responded to questions in the Grand Jury had Joel Jacobs not pulled me out when he did? What if that rookie detective had not compiled the report confirming my phone call to the Deputy Commissioner after the penitentiary riot? I had been told that representing Beauvais was a career ending mistake. What if it really had been? I was always on the edge of being fired but made it to the end through it all. Doing what I considered to be the right thing placed me in jeopardy frequently, but I also think it's what made me strong. When confronted with difficult choices, I always asked. What is the right thing to do? Not the easiest, or the safest, but what is right? I think Uncle Jerry and Grandpa George would be proud.

My move to Florida was accomplished quickly. I spent several months stocking my freezer with game fish I caught and once again getting my pool game back to a more than respectable level. I bought a boat that would get me offshore of Florida's east coast and went fishing every morning. I would play pool in the afternoon, making enough money to cover most of my recreational needs. Days lost meaning after a short while. Doing the same thing every day felt like the endless loop in "Groundhog Day". I decided to get a job, but I needed to do one more thing before getting tied down.

I packed up my Harley Davidson Roadglide and headed out without a plan. I visited my Navy buddy Jack in upstate New York, my friend Jean in Ohio, the Blue Ridge Mountains, and Graceland. One month and 5,000 miles later, I returned to Florida.

Upon return, I began exploring the types of jobs available to me. Though I was retired, I was only 50 years old. I didn't need money, but raising my standard of living and keeping busy would be nice. Armed security would pay the most money without undue responsibility. I already had my concealed weapons license for Florida, but armed security requires a dedicated license. The class D license was a simple matter of a written test and live fire at a range. I aced the written test, and after my target was scored, the range instructor commented,

"I take it you've done this before."

I eventually applied for the position, Superintendent of a live-in Juvenile Diversion Program. I could never pass up a challenge and this sounded like one. This job was ideally suited to my qualifications and should be easy compared to my previous employment. My resume impressed, and I was hired in short order. The juvenile diversion program at this point was only on paper.

Carlos Garcia, my boss, was a Cuban-born American who had submitted a grant that the state government had approved. I was not a state employee; I worked for Carlos since he held the grant. Carlos was a brilliant man who made a career writing grants. He told me he had a similar operation in Miami, about 50 miles away. I was starting from scratch, however, and there needed to be a model to follow. The plan was to find a suitable structure that could be renovated and build the program from the ground up. Carlos was an easygoing guy, and I would work independently most of the time.

Carlos identified a structure already owned by the state of Florida, a vacant two-story building with a sizeable tract of land. Carlos said he had hired a contractor to clear and level the land to erect greenhouses for cultivating exotic fruit trees. I didn't see that in the grant, but the boss was writing the checks, so it was fine by me.

Renovation was the first order of business. Then, I was to hire staff, develop training criteria, and create the program. The first hires would be an assistant superintendent then teachers, followed by the security staff and counselors. Florida has stringent laws on the control and restraining of juveniles.

All staff, including myself, would have to take state-run training as a condition of employment. The restraining techniques I relied upon during my last career were strictly prohibited. Various techingues taught to police such as pain control were prohibited under the law. Instead, takedowns and restraining techniques, presumably risking more harm to the custodian, were taught and practiced. We were expecting first-offenders, so I could live with the "kid gloves" approach, at least that's what I thought initially.

It took several months to complete the renovation and begin hiring. Since some of our budget expenditure was close to maxing out, I chipped in my labor after hours. I built shelves where needed and even a few weatherproof ping pong tables for the recreation yard. The land around the building had been cleared, and now greenhouses were being constructed out back. Carlos was handling all aspects related to the outdoor construction. I was concerned how this related to our program but assumed I would be read in at some point.

Everything was coming together on time, and I was told within budget. I never saw the budget, which was frankly one less headache. I began hiring teachers, counselors, and, most importantly, a competent assistant superintendent.

With everything in place, I met with the state Juvenile Justice authorities to discuss the juveniles to be diverted to our program. I also met with the Lantana Chief of Police, to fully brief him on our mission.

The grant expressly stated we were to get nonviolent and low-risk first offenders. No locks on living quarters were allowed, so escape would be as simple as walking away. Every juvenile must attend school on-site. It was agreed that any refusals, violations of rules, or inappropriate behavior would be cause for removal. Everything was in place. What could go wrong?

We received the first two juveniles into our fledgling diversion program. It was a celebration, and everyone turned out. John was a giant, angry 15-year-old, and William, Willy as he preferred, was a slight 14-year-old who refused to wear shoes. John had a long history of violent behavior, which he demonstrated by destroying the classroom on the first day.

He so traumatized the teacher that she resigned before completing even one full school day. The remaining teachers voiced concern about what they were led to believe upon being hired. It was confirmed early on that Willy had a long history of running away. He did so the second day.

Citing noncompliance with the grant, I called for a meeting with Juvenile Justice Authorities. Their response was,

"This is what you get. There are no first or nonviolent offenders available."

According to authorities, I had received the cream of the crop. From day one, I struggled to keep staff and maintain order. We received a few more juveniles into the program as chaos ensued

Over the next two weeks, John refused to attend class, and Willy ran away twice, though he came back each time. The building was a two-story with a false third-floor dome at one end. Living quarters were on the second floor, and my office, classrooms, and other administrative spaces were on the first floor. All first-floor spaces opened to the outside.

I was in my office when a counselor came running in.

"Mr. Kenney, come outside. You gotta see this."

I went outside and looked to the top of the building where the counselor was pointing. Willy was sitting on top of the dome three stories above the ground.

"How did he get up there?"

"Sir, he went up the side of the building like a squirrel."

I was faced with a difficult dilemma. Options raced through my mind. Calling the fire department seemed like the responsible option. However, I feared it could endanger Willy even more, and there was adverse publicity to be considered. I could imagine the fire engines, sirens, and inflatable bags in case he jumped or fell. Newspaper headlines would certainly doom the program.

'Maybe I can end this quietly,' I thought to myself.

If he could get up there, hopefully he could get down. I ushered the counselor inside so Willy would not have the attention he was seeking.

I yelled to Willy, "Hey Willy, come to my office when you can, I need to talk to you about something."

I then casually walked back to my office and nervously waited for either his arrival or the untimely death of a fourteen-year-old child due to my dismissive response.

Leaving Willy to his own devices to get down from the roof was, in hindsight, irresponsible. I wish I had made a less passive decision. Fortunately, it did work out. It wasn't more than a few minutes later when Willy walked in with a big grin on his face. He was a cute kid, and he was soaking up the attention. If I made a big deal about his building climbing he would do it again, so I didn't even mention it.

We had no way of controlling the likes of John and Willy, and I told Carlos that we had three choices: 1. Add physical controls such as locked doors, extra staff, and consequences for rules violations 2. Hold Juvenile Justice to the letter of the grant regarding first offender status, behavior, and cooperation, or 3. Cancel the program before someone got hurt.

Carlos proposed a different option. Another location had been acquired in a portion of a state-owned building as a secure lockup for problem detainees. Both facilities would be maintained. I would continue to be in charge of one, and a superintendent from the Miami facility would be brought in to run the other. Since the budget would become a problem, some of my staff, including my assistant superintendent, would have to go.

I was being kept in the dark regarding several items. The fruit tree farm was becoming a significant concern. How did that figure into anything? I surmised the Miami facility may have had similar problems as they would be drawing from the same group of juveniles. The incident with Willy climbing to the top of the building shook me. The juveniles referred to the program needed a structured environment and were unsuited to our program. I feared severe injury would result.

One day, Carlos showed up with Stefanie, his Miami superintendent, and four other staff members. Carlos showed them into a vacant office without introduction. They worked out of this office for several days without so much as a "good morning".

At this point, I had severe reservations about the dishonesty of juvenile justice dumping problems into our program, contrary to the specifications in the grant. It was also apparent that my boss was making deals behind my back, and keeping important matters from me..

I could not understand why an exotic fruit tree farm was being built as part of the facility. The program budget was hidden from me. I filed financial reports on monies spent and bills that would be paid or expenditures reimbursed, but there was little accountability, which, in light of all the other issues, began to concern me.

The latest changes were doomed to fail due to staff cuts and overall uncertainty. I had based the program on information in the grant that no longer applied. The superintendent and other staff Carlos brought in from Miami suggested the Miami program had ended, meaning I'd been lied to.

That was the final straw. I would have preferred to stay on and work on the problem, but I was no longer in control. I cited the untenable conditions and gave my two weeks' notice. I was overcome with guilt. I felt like I was bailing at a critical moment. Carlos didn't seem surprised and maybe a little relieved.

He may have been happy to make room for his Miami superintendent. This was a monumental failure because I did not take a stand when I knew I should have. The building and quality controls were lacking, and I should have stood up to Carlos. The Juvenile Authorities did not keep to the terms of the grant, and I should have stood up to them. I realized my entire approach to this position and the resulting problems were out of character for me. Warden Kenney never would have accepted the ever-changing criteria, the shifty boss, reneging on agreed to terms- none of it.

I quickly decided to look for another job. I did not want to spend time brooding over this disappointment. I promised myself I would look for something with less responsibility. I was stressed out. Even all these years later, I was still dealing with PTSD, and I was embarrassed over this failure. Getting another job right away would be good therapy, I told myself. I will take my time to explore my options and not grab the first thing that comes along. Yeah, right!

Playing pool for extra money was always an option. I still played every day and it had been therapeutic.

Playing pool at a high level requires intense concentration. All the clutter in the brain must be removed in order to reach the necessary level of focus. Top pool players call it "The Zone". Focus becomes so acute that the game becomes easy and the player controls the outcome. It is a state of mind that is elusive to most and difficult to achieve even by professional players. To a few, including myself, it is easily switched on or off. 'The Zone', that feeling of clarity and flow, is my main attraction to the game. When I am playing there is nothing else. I shut out everything- good, bad, and ugly. I exist in the game. It has always been my escape.

The first item that caught my attention in the Help Wanted column of the newspaper was an ad for "Security Manager, at an International Airport."

No telephone number, just: "Apply Concourse B checkpoint".

No harm in checking it out, I thought. I liked the idea of working around aircraft again.

I arrived at the airport just after noon and proceeded to the B concourse. A uniformed security supervisor at the checkpoint advised me that I had just missed the "Boss" and I should return at 9am the next day.

The airport was bustling, and a long line of people were waiting to pass through security. I noticed that USA Airline and a few smaller airlines used Concourse B. I walked down to C Concourse, which was used primarily by Beta Air Lines, American, and Continental Airlines. Here, three long lines were waiting to enter the metal detectors. I thought back to when I was fresh out of the Navy and applied to an airline, only to be humiliated. Still, I wanted to give it a shot.

Bright and early the following day, I was ushered into a small office cubicle adjacent to the passenger metal detectors. It was a tiny area, barely large enough for a desk, two chairs, and a few file cabinets. Peter Colson, Vice President of Global Total Services, a firm contracted to run the checkpoint for USA Airline, would interview me. Peter was a retired New York City detective with a personality to match that role. We got along quite well immediately. I knew my resume could be impressive to potential employers, but Peter had "been there, done that".

He understood better than most the skills I might offer. We spoke the same language. We had done some of the same things, like attending the same FBI training sessions, and knew some of the same people.

Keeping with his New York demeanor, Peter was quick to the point. My job, if accepted, would be to manage the passenger security checkpoint. It would include ensuring compliance with FAA rules, hiring and training staff, and, most importantly, keeping the client happy.

"I am going to be honest with you," Peter said. "We have had problems with this checkpoint. I just let the previous manager go. I have a salary range for this position. I would like to bring you in at the top of that range.

"My plane leaves in an hour, so I need your answer now."

With little thought, I said, "I'll take the job Peter, I'm up for the challenge."

This was in 1993, well before 9/11, which catapulted the reality of airline security into the headlines. Instead, this was a time when security checkpoint screeners were paid a minimum wage of $4.15 an hour. Devoid of all pertinent information regarding this position, I said yes with little thought to the consequences. With roughly twenty employees to whip into shape, I would have six months to straighten things out before the contract came up for renewal. Even if I achieved the task, USA Airline could still opt for a different security firm when that time came. What the hell? Can't be worse than my last job.

Peter called Betty in from the checkpoint and introduced her.

"Betty has been temporarily running the checkpoint. She is the day shift supervisor."

Betty scowled, "Nice to meet you."

I immediately sensed that Betty felt I was infringing on her authority and possible promotion to manager. Next, we visited the USA Airline offices. The USA Ailine Manager, Beth Palmer was attractive, articulate, and direct. In his introduction, Peter built me up as the perfect person to correct all problems at the checkpoint.

Beth spoke slowly and purposely as if she wanted me to understand every word thoughtfully chosen.

"Fred, I would like to work closely with you on this. You will have my full support. I am sure Peter has informed you about the problems we have experienced at the checkpoint."

I assured Beth that I was on the job and would work diligently to bring the checkpoint up to the highest standard.

Upon returning to the checkpoint office cubicle, Peter pointed to a bookshelf containing several three-ring binders.

"In those binders is everything you need to know about checkpoint regulations and procedures governed by the FAA. Study and memorize them. If you do everything that is in them, you can't go wrong. I'll check back here in a couple of weeks."

Peter Colson was a regional vice president in charge of all the airports in the southeast United States where "GTS" had security and other airline service contracts. He raced off to catch his flight. A little over an hour ago, I had applied for a job. Now I'm responsible for the safety of thousands of airline passengers boarding numerous flights every day.

Chapter 10

FLORIDAFRED

After a rough start in Florida, I was settling into my new management position. Ensuring safety for the traveling public addressed my need to serve. There was a popular poolroom only a mile from the airport where I could make some extra money and relax from the stress of work. Through all my varied employment experiences, the one constant was the game of pool. It was a comfortable world I could always slip into, no matter the tumult I felt elsewhere.

I entered my first 9 ball tournament since moving to Florida. The venue was a poolroom two hours drive from my home. I was happy to see two old friends upon arrival, Larry, and Steve Mizerak. Larry explained that he had a guy he was backing in the tournament and was hoping to make some backroom money. Sadly, he told me Sammy had been shot and killed a few months ago.

"Sammy got involved in some things he shouldn't have," was all he would say.

I had always felt safe in poolrooms, but there is a dark side and the opportunity at times to take the wrong path.

"Everybody's moving to Florida, I had to follow the money," Larry said.

Steve Mizerak greeted me, "Hey, it's New York, Fred; what are you doing here?"

I explained that I had moved to Florida.

Steve replied, "Well, me too, so now you're, Floridafred."

The name stuck.

I started out strong, winning my first three matches. Next, however, I would be playing Tommy Kennedy, one of the circuit's nicest guys, but more importantly, one of its best players. Tommy did not fit the typical pool player mold. He did not gamble, and he would not curse. Tommy had a smile and a greeting for everyone.

Tommy won the US 9 ball Open some years ago. The US Open attracts two hundred and fifty-six of the best pool players from all over the world. Winning that event puts you in a class with very few other players.

We were in a race to nine for a chance to play in the finals. I had just evened the score at eight to eight, we were both on the hill. It was my break. I broke the rack, making four balls on the break. The one ball hung in the pocket, making for an easy runout. As luck would have it, the cue ball wedged between the rail and the three ball, making a shot at the one ball impossible. I could not kick, jump or masse' the shot. I tried a masse' kick in desperation, but Tommy received ball in hand and ran out the game.

Tommy was apologetic in his win. "Wow, tough break Fred."

Luckily, it was a double elimination tournament, but if I lost one more match, I would be on my way home.

I heard the announcement sealing my fate.

"Floridafred and Miami Al, table six."

As I approached the table Al was already practicing.

Alphonse "Miami Al" Montoya was a charismatic, well-dressed player displaying an arrogant confidence. He wore a cream colored, Cuban style shirt with matching slacks and Fedora. While I'd never witnessed his expertise on the pool table firsthand, tales had circulated about his exceptional skill in high-stakes pool games.

He was accompanied by his girlfriend Isabelle. The crowd was already gathering around the table to 'watch the game', but most eyes were on Isabelle. She was perched in the one chair designated as the "Player Chair". It had a high seat and footrest to afford the player a comfortable and commanding view of the table on which he was playing.

Al lacked the sportsmanship to ask his girlfriend to move so I could take my seat, and I was too much of a gentleman to protest. I stood for the entire match and watched as Isabelle would shudder with glee and silently clap her hands every time Al won a game. When it was my time at the table, Al and Isabelle talked and petted each other in a tawdry distraction. I exited swiftly after losing the match to avoid putting my anger on display.

"Taking Heat" is a poolroom term for the conspicuous emotional depression one goes through after a disappointing loss. I was still taking heat for both losses at the tournament when I walked into Palm Coast Billiards in West Palm Beach. The only way to dissipate that heat is to have a big win, and that's what I was looking for.

Milo the "Claw" was practicing on a table in "The Pit". Though at the time, I had no knowledge of either him or "The Pit".

Milo had a very unique style of play. Steve Mizerak said he looked like a lobster claw when he was shooting. As with most of Steve's pronouncements, the name stuck. Milo was a big man in his forties who understood and played the game better than most. Lee, Milo's girlfriend, was always in attendance. She was attractive, Asian, friendly, and very rich. While Milo would play for hours, Lee would sit off to the side reading or attending to other personal matters. She was never a distraction like Isabelle had been at the tournament.

The Pit was an area in the middle of the poolroom containing a pool table and two player's chairs. You had to step down into the pit because it was a foot lower than the rest of the floor. It was surrounded by a railing with seating and tables for onlookers, or in poolroom jargon, "Rail Birds". The table was a Brunswick Gold Crown with narrow pockets reminiscent of Toby's practice table. I was at the top of my game, so tight pockets were no longer a problem.

I watched Milo play for a short period of time, then asked him if he would like to play some 9 ball. We agreed on a friendly game of races to seven for fifty dollars. Milo was good, but I managed to win four close sets. Milo was also from New York and was familiar with the West End and all the other pool rooms in New York. We struck up a friendly conversation which revealed how much we had in common. We knew the same people and we had both been in the West End Poolroom at the exact same time on several occasions. It's a big room and always crowded so it's not unusual we had not met.

Milo introduced me to Lee who was instantly likeable, though they seemed like an odd couple. Milo was rough in speech and in dress. Lee was well spoken, dressed casually but very neat and pressed. She was obviously very intelligent, Milo, not so. The three of us got a table in the restaurant section to continue our conversation.

"Want some pizza?" Milo asked.

"Sure, why not."

Milo called out, "Hey, can we get some damn service over here?"

A man came to our table and engaged Milo in heated conversation that sounded Greek to me. In fact, it turned out to indeed be Greek, a native tongue which both Milo and Alex spoke.

They both laughed and Milo said, "This is Alex, the manager."

"Nice to meet you," and he went off to get our pizza and some beers.

Milo knew, Larry, Sammy, Black Dave, and other familiar players.

Milo had driven a cab in New York City and played pool mostly in Queens before moving to Florida.

"Do you know who owns this poolroom?" Milo asked.

"I don't know, I suppose maybe Alex."

"No, Alex's just the manager, Larry owns the poolroom."

"Wow, he never mentioned that to me, when does he come in?"

"Never, it's kind of a secret."

"Hey, did you hear about Toby?" Milo said.

"What about him? Every poolroom in New York has a Toby Story, but I've never met him."

"Well, he's in Florida now, and last week he played Miami Al for a hundred grand.

"A hundred thousand dollars." I wanted to be sure I heard him right.

"Yea, Toby put up fifty thousand of his own money and Larry put up fifty thousand. With side bets there had to be at least two hundred thou' on the line.

"What did they play?"

"9 ball, race to thirty-five. It took two days.

"Wow, who won, what was the final score?"

"At the end of the first day Miami Al was ahead seventeen to Toby's eleven. What do you think the final score was?" he didn't wait for my reply, "Twenty-nine to thirty-five, Toby."

The mythical figure exists. I had heard so many Toby stories in varied poolrooms and from such a wide-ranging cast of characters I thought he might be a made-up folk hero. I thought of Isabelle and her silent clapping when her man won. I felt bad, she was probably sad. No, wait, the thought actually made me feel pretty good.

We were getting ready to leave and I asked Milo, "Wanna to play some next week?"

"Sure, but this poolroom won't be here."

"It's closing?"

"Yea, Alex is going to open his own poolroom in Lantana. Same tables, Larry is backing him. I'll call and let you know the date. We gotta make a good showing for the opening."

"Yeah, I'll be there for sure."

The check came and Lee reached for it. Since I had won a couple hundred dollars, I felt obliged to pay.

"I'll get it," I said to Lee.

Milo interrupted, "Don't be stupid, she could buy the whole block."

I let Lee get the check.

I showed up for the opening of Alex's new pool room. It was located in a busy shopping center at the intersection of two main roads. It was a storefront with the large windows blacked out to prevent the sun and glare of headlights interfering with play. There were ten pool tables and two billiard tables. A small kitchen served mostly cold food- tasty sandwiches with freshly sliced deli meats, beer, and soda. It was much nicer than the room where I first met Milo.

Nobody was playing pool, even though there was a large crowd present. Two pool tables had protective covers with a spread of catered food covering both. There was free soda and beer could be purchased.

I observed Milo and Lee conversing with a small group and joined in. I met Danny and Rocco at Milo's introduction.

Milo said, "Rocco, you and Fred are a good game, but Danny needs the eight ball unless you play straight pool, then it might be even."

Milo was interrupted by a thunderous rumble that shook the poolroom. A car had pulled up close to the windows. The driver seemed to be taunting those in the poolroom. With each rev, the powerful engine sent vibrations through the air, creating an intense growl you could feel in your stomach.

Milo yelled out, "Toby's here!"

The engine noise stopped, and I immediately fixed my eyes on the entrance. After decades of tall tales, I was finally going to meet Toby.

I wondered if the description I had heard so many times would be accurate. Some of the stories I heard had no name attached but identified him by an unmistakable description. He was thin, with long blonde hair and he always wore bell bottom pants.

The door opened and in he walked. He stopped a few feet inside the door to allow his eyes to adjust to the dim light. After that moment he continued to the tumultuous greetings and even applause. He had vanquished Miami Al with his mighty cue stick. I even felt he had struck that blow for me.

Toby was thin, maybe five foot eight, in his forties, with long dirty blonde hair down to his shoulders. He carried a cue case and wore his trademark bellbottom pants. Where do you even get them these days? The description I had heard in so many pool rooms was spot on accurate.

After the festivities died down I was sitting at a table with Milo, Toby, Alex, and Lee. Milo introduced me to Toby by saying that the first time we met I had hustled him out of two hundred dollars.

"Oh yeah, that's my kind of guy," Toby said.

Milo said, "Toby, chirp down that big game for us."

"Chirp" being a blow-by-blow description of a game.

"It was no big deal; Larry had the biggest share of the money. I put up fifty grand and Larry put up fifty, but then Larry had another fifty or sixty in side bets."

I told Toby about my tournament match with Miami Al.

"Yeah, he's a piece of shit and so is his girl. She was doing a lot of clapping on the first day, but I shut them up on day two."

"Who made the game?" Milo asked.

"Larry made the initial approach, but I hammered out the details. I wanted a long game, the longer I play the better I play, while the competition gets tired. After the first day he only had me by a few games, so the pressure was off. I knew I had him."

Toby said, "Hey Fred, you wanna play a few games of 9 ball for five a game? I'll give you the six ball."

"Sure, I'll play but I don't need a spot."

"Yeah, you do. C'mon."

When we got to the table, I again told Toby I didn't want the spot. At five a game I couldn't get hurt too bad. I relished the opportunity to play this legend, particularly after he won a match for a hundred grand. Now he's playing for five dollars.

"Look Fred, the five dollars is just to keep it sociable and the 6 ball is because I can't play unless it's uphill for me. So do me a favor and take the six."

After an hour or so we broke even. He would effortlessly run four and five racks at a time while carrying on a conversation. Great player that he was, his game was simple. He did not do anything that I couldn't replicate.

Consistency was what made him so good. He rarely did anything fancy with the cue ball. He would hit the cueball dead center ninety five percent of the time. He would make the object ball with the cue ball taking a natural path to the next object ball. Sometimes it was a long shot and sometimes a short one, but he always had the right angle to get on the next ball and he just did not miss.

Spotting me the 6 ball meant if I made the 9 ball or the six ball I would win. Toby would win only by making the 9 ball. This gave me a tremendous advantage and even with that leverage I could do no better than break even.

I played Milo a couple times a week after Alex's place opened. We bet twenty dollars a set just to keep the game interesting, but we had become good friends and didn't want to take the other's money.

One day between sets Milo had gone for a break, Lee called out to me.

"Fred," she beckoned to me. "Come and look at this," she said, holding up her checkbook. "This is a crying shame."

"What is it, Lee?"

I walked over to where she was sitting. She was pointing to the check she had just made out, still in her checkbook.

"Can you believe I have to pay this much money? It's robbery."

Lee was pointing to a check made out to the IRS for two hundred and fifty thousand dollars.

Wow, if you pay that much imagine what you get to keep.

"Lee, that is a crying shame", I said

When I was playing in the tournaments, I started carrying a small camera with me and I took a few portrait style photos of friends. Using sophisticated software on my computer, I developed a process to give the images a dramatic black and white painterly look. I printed the portraits on a sixteen by twenty canvas board. The first time I brought one to the pool room everybody wanted one. I began selling them for one hundred and fifty dollars each and I sold dozens of them.

I made up a few copies for Toby and planned to gift them to him. I also made up several extras for him to autograph. I figured we could sell them for five hundred apiece and split the money. After all, he was a legend.

When I told Toby I'd bring them to the poolroom, he said, "No, bring them to my apartment, I want to show you something."

According to Toby's directions, I had to park in a certain area and then walk a hundred yards or so. I didn't realize until I got close to his front door that his apartment was right on the Intercoastal Waterway in Palm Beach. His front door opened onto a dock.

It was a small apartment very simply furnished. Upon entering the living room, I noticed the walls crowded with paintings. There were also canvases stacked against the wall.

"What's with all the paintings?" I asked.

"I painted them all, what do you think?"

"Damn Toby, they're really good. do you sell them?"

"No, I don't, do you think I could?"

"Sure, if you had a place to exhibit them, I'm sure you could sell some."

I gave Toby the three portraits I had done of him plus the extras to be sold.

"Sign the rest of them and I'll try to sell them for five hundred each, we'll split the money fifty, fifty."

Toby said, "No, you keep the money, you did all the work."

"Ok, we'll see." If I were to sell any I would repay Toby in some way.

I handed Toby a gold marker I had brought along for his signature on the black background of the prints.

"No, I can't sign, I print." Toby said.

"No problem, print is good." I was thinking he probably quit school at an early age like me.

On each canvas in turn Toby printed his name in block letters.

"Hey, I got something else I've gotta show you." He hurried into another room and quickly returned with a pile of papers. He plopped them down in front of me. "Tell me what you think."

There were loose papers and an assortment of notebooks filled with that very neat block printing.

"Toby, what is this?"

"Mostly poetry that I wrote but some short stories, what do you think? Here, read this one."

l read from the loose piece of paper he passed to me. It was a full-page poem, very well crafted and obviously the product of a creative mind. I revisited the opinion I had formulated when Toby told me he couldn't sign but had to print.

There were notebooks filled with his writings. Poems were written on the backs of envelopes and scraps of paper. Short stories about pool characters, some unfinished works. The more I learned about Toby, the more mysterious and multifaceted he became.

"Hey Fred, do you have a boat?"

"No, I don't, I sold mine. Why?"

"I have a sixty-foot boat slip that comes with this apartment, but I don't have a boat."

"Fucking unbelievable, you're paying for a sixty-foot slip and you don't even have a boat."

"Yeah, it's crazy. But if I bought a sixty-foot boat then I wouldn't need the apartment."

"Yeah, that makes sense," I said.

Chapter 11

AIRLINE SECURITY

O nce again, I had taken on a challenging position likely destined for failure. My company had been informed that immediate improvements must be made, or the contract wouldn't be renewed. Problems before my arrival put this airline and its security checkpoint on the Federal Aviation Administration's hit list. It was now up to me to correct those problems, and I had little time to do it. Those retirees bagging groceries at Publix, are the smart ones. Why couldn't I be satisfied with something like that?

The realization of my responsibilities and the task ahead was suddenly overwhelming. Panic was setting in. I had to make this work. What would Warden Kenney do? The first step in dealing with any overwhelming project is to break it down into smaller components, prioritize the most essential elements, and then attack them one at a time.

It was still a daunting task, but the outcome would not be left to chance. Renewal of the contract was not my only goal. My immediate priority had to be the safety of the traveling public. This checkpoint had not met minimum security standards for a long time and that needed to change. The mechanism for providing safe, secure travel was not up to me; it was spelled out in considerable detail by Federal Aviation Administration directives. My priority was to know those directives better than the FAA and get them implemented as quickly as possible.

The FAA put a detailed system of pre board screening in place to be followed by the airlines with severe consequence for noncompliance. The FAA procedures covering checkpoint security were contained in the three notebooks that Peter had pointed out to me. The first days of my employment were spent studying the regulations contained in those notebooks. I came to understand the mandates for running a security checkpoint better than any FAA agent, but implementing the procedures would be a race against time.

The FAA required the person training new hires to take a three-day certification course. Having no choice, I flew out to Maryland during my first week on the job to get my certification. The course was a compressed version of the five-day course given to new screeners, but it gave no insight into how to train, why to train, or tips on methods, so its usefulness was limited at best. The instructor simply read from a prepared lesson plan and would not answer questions.

"Everything is in the handouts," was the answer to any question.

The trip to Maryland was a waste of time and money. They could have just sent me the lesson plan. The required one-week training had nothing to do with operating the x-ray machine or magnetometer. It had nothing to do with proper search of passengers or the intrapersonal skills required to accomplish these delicate practices.

Even so, my first two objectives were accomplished within my first week of employment. I was certified to train new hires and I had a good understanding of the FAA requirements for checkpoint operations. My next priority would be to evaluate the checkpoint operation and bring it up to standard. I placed an ad for security screeners in the help wanted section of the local paper. I needed to start a class for new screeners as soon as I could.

Betty, the checkpoint supervisor Peter had introduced me to, was running the checkpoint with a false notion of self-confidence. She displayed little regard for the employees and treated them disrespectfully. Her early advice to me was to stay out of the way and let her handle things.

I wrestled with the thought of how I might re-educate her as a supervisor. I needed every employee and could not afford to lose any, but her methods and attitude did not fit what I needed to accomplish. It is critical to treat employees with respect while providing the tools and knowledge to accomplish their jobs. Unfortunately, I had scheduled interviews for new screeners and planned on starting a class within a week. That would take me away from the checkpoint for five days. I had little choice but to do as Betty suggested—stay out of her way and let her manage things while I was teaching a class.

My plan to simply observe the checkpoint for now was short lived. I'd observed the checkpoint for less than twenty minutes before I jumped in with both feet. Betty waved a man around security, allowing him to enter the concourse without being screened.

"Sir, please come back and go through security."

The man came back indignantly as I directed him to get into line.

Betty hurriedly approached me, "I know him, he's a vendor on the concourse, he can go.

"No, he can't, there are no exceptions, everyone goes through security."

"You can't do this, you're going to get yourself in trouble," Betty said.

Betty was completely oblivious to most of the rules and was playing fast and loose with the few she was aware of. Within the next few hours of my supposed 'observations', I made enemies of countless persons not used to going through the security process. Department of Airport supervisors and management were accustomed to bypassing security. I put a stop to that.

Pilots were required to go through security, but Betty gave them a pass. They would carry their flight bag and alarm the magnetometer to be waived on without being checked.

The first pilot I insisted be properly screened made quite a scene in front of his passengers.

"Why would I need a weapon!?" he yelled, "I could just crash the fucking plane and kill everybody."

It did not take long for a supervisor from the Department of Airports to seek me out.

"What the hell are you doing?" he said.

"Good morning, I'm Fred Kenney, Security Checkpoint manager and you are?"

"Dave Goodman, supervisor, Department of Airports, what are you doing? I'm getting all kinds of complaints."

"Well Mr. Goodman, the FAA has had concerns regarding checkpoint security, so I've been brought in to ensure compliance with FAA regulations."

Mr. Goodman stormed off without further comment. His lack of social skills indicated to me that he had no idea how to react to my command of the checkpoint. He obviously had to seek guidance from someone higher up.

I purposely invoked the FAA term as it was their authority that I was relying on. I knew I was making waves and Betty was enjoying the condemnation I was getting from all corners of the airport. Here I was once more fighting a system, making enemies, and preparing to stand up to the FAA, Airport Management, and possibly my boss. The alternative would be to accept a failed system.

The Department of Airports is the landlord that runs the physical building and rents out space to various airlines and vendors doing business at the airport. There is a long list of supervisors in charge of various organizational functions who represent them. The DOA is a bureaucracy, political in nature, and difficult to navigate. The personnel department complicates my hiring of staff with their ever-changing criteria.

I was not surprised when I was summoned to Beth Palmer's office. As the USA Airline Manager responsible for the checkpoint, she would be the one to sign off on the contract renewal. If she went against me, I was toast.

Beth was a young woman in the male dominated domain of airline managers. She was strikingly attractive with short blonde hair and a captivating smile. She garnered attention and respect the moment she stepped into a room. Her attire, always perfectly tailored, complemented her shapely form. She would not only be noticed but remembered. Beyond her physical appearance, her articulate speech and confident demeanor marked her as a leader and someone to be reckoned with.

"Well Fred, it is apparent that everyone knows you're here," Beth smiled.

"Growing pains Beth, it may be a little bumpy until I get things straightened out."

"Does this mean I have to go through security also?" Beth said.

"I'm afraid so."

"I'm with you Fred, just be aware that you're making enemies, so be on solid ground."

"Beth, our main concern has to be the FAA. All of my efforts are to comply with their mandates. Once I get caught up on that front, we will be fine."

"Thank you, Fred. Keep me informed."

I told Beth we would be fine, but I had my concerns. I was needed at the checkpoint to ensure my security program would be applied consistently. Betty could not handle it and I was convinced she would do whatever necessary to weaken my position. Now was the time to stand strong and face down any opposition.

Beth was on my side, but I would have to earn her trust and support over the next few months. The checkpoint was a mess, which meant I had a long way to go. I was spread too thin. I could not simultaneously recruit, train, retrain, and manage the checkpoint. If I worked to fix one problem, two more would pop up behind my back.

I needed to hire fifteen new screeners to fully staff the checkpoint. The screeners I did have needed to be retrained; some were beyond help. It was vital to know every screener's capability, strengths, and weaknesses. Betty, the supervisor, was a tyrant and she was not on my side. I would have to replace her.

Martin was a screener that caught my attention. His round face, often lit up with a smile, and the jovial twang of his Jamaican accent added a layer of warmth to his personality. He wore his uniform with pride, and he was looked upon by his peers as a leader. He possessed a unique blend of qualities that impressed me. Martin's intelligence was clear, though his misunderstandings of local customs and language nuances sometimes led to moments of awkwardness. These moments were far outweighed by his relentless effort to please and his competence in the tasks at hand. His loyalty was beyond question, always addressing me with a respectful, "Boss Man".

"Martin, my name is Fred, call me Fred."

"Yes, Mr. Fred, boss mon."

Sandy was another screener who caught my attention. She was a large woman in her mid-twenties who was competent and outspoken, more like loud. Sandy's voice had the unmistakable cultural linguistics of a Florida redneck. Her words were often loud but infused with a warmth that was hard to ignore. She had already mastered the nuances of her screening role, displaying a level of competence and a willingness to assist that set her apart from others. Her suggestions spoke volumes of her innate problem-solving skills. It was her uncanny ability to identify and address issues before they escalated that really caught my attention.

We were due for an FAA test or inspection, the results of which could be disastrous. We were not ready. I worried about the viability of the checkpoint under the current conditions. Reality had set in, I needed to take a bold step. I called Peter Colson, Vice President of Global Total Services, my employer.

"Peter, I need a dedicated trainer and a dedicated assistant manager."

"Sorry Fred, it's not in the budget."

"Peter, I've only got a few months to straighten this place out, and I'm spread too thin. I can't be everywhere at once. We have a future in this airport, and I can make it happen. But right now, I need help."

There was no reply. I broke the uncomfortable silence.

"Without those positions, we're going to lose this contract and any future growth potential."

I knew I was putting everything on the line, confronting Peter like this.

I continued, "Look Peter, eat the cost for a few months and build the cost into the new contract when USA Airline renews. With the proper tools I can make this work."

That was all I had, so I waited for the response.

It finally came, "OK Fred, do it."

I got right to work; I called Betty into the checkpoint office.

"Betty, I'm sorry, I'm letting you go. I will give you two weeks' severance pay."

I didn't have authorization to provide severance pay, but I figured I'd keep her on the books for two more weeks. Betty made it easy for me by replying,

"Good, I don't need this shit. You're going to lose the contract anyway."

"I'm sorry you feel that way, you can leave now."

Next, I called my Jamaican screener Martin in.

"Martin, how would you like to be the supervisor of the checkpoint and handle screener scheduling for me?"

"Yaw boss mon," was his enthusiastic response.

As Martin left the office he turned and said, "And thank you for getting rid of that witch, she made me miserable."

I thought to myself, 'Yeah, me too.'

Then, it was Sandy's turn.

"Sandy, I would like you to be the official trainer for this company; if you say yes, you take the first flight out tomorrow morning to Maryland and three days of training."

"Wow, definitely, yes, thank you so much, I won't let you down," she replied.

As fate would have it, I had interviews scheduled for new screeners that very day. My first interview, Mike Thorne walked into the cubicle. At first, I thought he must be an FAA Agent. He was impeccably dressed in tan slacks, a blue blazer, white shirt and tie, even a pocket handkerchief.

"I would like to apply for the screener position, sir," he said with a British accent.

He handed me a folder with his resume and sufficient documents for a fast background check.

I said, "You do realize this is minimum wage, don't you?"

"Yes sir," He replied.

"You are by far overqualified for the position. You do understand that?"

"Yes sir, I believe I just need to get my foot in the door."

"Well, Mike, I have one final question; how would you like to be my assistant manager?"

"Yes sir, I would like that very much."

"Your foot is in the door, Mike."

I had assembled my team. Martin, Sandy, and Mike were the tools I would use as an artist might to craft my masterpiece. It was incumbent upon me to share with them my vision for the checkpoint and beyond. Even more important was developing the individual character traits each possessed to get us there.

I worked closely with Martin at the checkpoint. It wasn't enough for him to understand and enforce the rules. I was interested in building a team that took pride in doing the important work we did. This wasn't just a job but a service to the traveling public in order to keep them safe.

Martin wore his uniform with pride. He was the only one that had a complete uniform.

"Boss mon, I had to buy my own shirts, we cannot get uniforms, look at these people, they look terrible."

It was a ragtag group at best. Many wore various colored sweaters to combat the cool temperature of the airport. I ordered complete uniforms, including sweaters, for all screeners and new hires.

I had to convince Martin to be a little more tolerant and patient with employees. He was quick to learn, eager to please, and loyal. His accent was charming, yet challenging to decipher when excitement got the better of him. This at times combined with cultural differences to hinder his ability to communicate effectively. Problems were rare however, and he became a very effective checkpoint supervisor.

Sandy proved to be more valuable than I could have imagined. She eagerly accepted her expanding responsibilities and took over all aspects of hiring new employee screeners. She did the background checks and even got along with the Airport personnel office. She turned out to be the perfect person for the job, even cutting down the time required for background checks. New hires had to be outfitted in uniform and she took over ordering and making sure everyone met Martin's uniform standard. The checkpoint was not only beginning to operate better, but it was also looking better.

For the first week I had Mike shadow me. As my assistant manager I wanted him to see how I manage the checkpoint. He would be free to develop his own style, however two points were of utmost importance to me. Number one, above all else was a strict adherence to the rules and regulations as set forth by the FAA. Number two was a family focused nurturing of employees. I wanted to develop a loyal, cohesive group that was proud of what they were doing. This is something you cannot mandate. We as managers have to set the conditions that allows it to happen. It is also important to recognize the difference between an employee that requires nurturing and one that simply does not belong.

Mike was the perfect fit. Once again, I had chosen wisely. I had initial concerns that since Mike was the new guy on the block there might be some resentment. Mike, to his credit, received immediate approval from all staff.

Martin hadn't felt the same way initially. He liked interacting with me directly and having another level of authority between us did not suit him. But once he realized I was not building a hierarchy everything leveled out.

I met with Sandy, Martin, and Mike at Starbucks on the concourse every morning. Peter Colson, Vice President of GTS had generously approved an expense account to be used at my discretion. These meetings were indispensable to my goals and were used for the same purpose as my morning briefings when I was Warden Kenney.

We would discuss the business of the day and what needed to be accomplished. A hot Vente Nonfat Latte was the timer for the length of the meeting. The majority of the time would be in casual conversation as friends and coworkers. Martin related funny stories about being employed as a policeman in Jamaica. Sandy always had something to say involving an alligator or a catfish. Mike's travels included the British Isles and India which made for interesting banter.

I was beginning to see those missing elements of loyalty and motivation blossom. I wanted to build a culture where employees felt they were appreciated for their contributions. Previously they had been beaten down by Airport Authorities, Sheriff's Deputies, the FAA, and their own employer. I would support them and earn their loyalty. Everything was beginning to fall into place. I just needed a little more time. But that was the one thing I didn't have.

A screener failed to detect a Hand Grenade test item placed into the x-ray machine by an FAA agent. The FAA agent, a young man named Roger, presumably new to the agency, had an inflated ego. He came into the office demanding that the screener be removed until he could be retrained. He also demanded to see all training records, background checks, test items, and the regulations in the out-of-date three-ring notebooks.

He was correct in his authority, but his attitude irked me. I called Beth at USA Airline, but she was in a meeting. I told her secretary we had failed an FAA test, and the checkpoint was being audited.

The agent was still conducting his audit an hour later when Beth entered the cubicle. She introduced herself to the agent and asked what the situation was. Roger stopped what he was doing,

"Well, you failed a test item, these regulations are a year behind, and you had too many test items in inventory. I'm in the process of going through the training records now."

The first few training records he reviewed were acceptable, as they were done recently. The older ones prior to my arrival would be a problem when he got to them. We had three hand grenade test items and two pipe bomb test items. We should have one of each item and an up-to-date inventory of all test items. The extra test items were a problem. How do you dispose of two hand grenades and a pipe bomb? They are inert of course, but they look real and could initiate an undesirable reaction.

The FAA agent was sitting at my desk in the cramped cubicle. There was only one other chair. Beth walked over and sat on the desk, one leg on the floor and the other draped over the side of the desk inches from the agent. Her tight-fitting dress hiked up high on her thigh.

She said, "Roger, as you probably know, we have had issues with this checkpoint. That is why we have brought in Mr. Kenney. He is an expert with a lot of experience, and given time, he assures me he can fix this problem. Why don't you and I go up to my office where I can take proper notes and set a time for your return to view the changes we will be making?"

Roger agreed, and they departed for Beth's office. I wondered if that had been an intentional move on Beth's part, to distract him before he got to the sub-par training records. The provocative bearing of her leg certainly seemed to draw his attention.

I was stressed out. I had no idea how Beth or my boss Peter was going to react to this failure and audit. I knew we had a lot of problems and praying for enough time to make improvements was not working. After an hour or so, I got a call that Beth wanted to see me in her office. As I ascended the escalator to her office behind the ticket counter, I expected she would be angry and want to get Peter the Vice President of GTS involved.

Beth caught my eye as I entered the outer office, and she beckoned me to come right in.

Beth spoke as I entered, "Wow, that guy was a piece of work, wasn't he?"

"He sure was," I replied.

Her opening line took me by complete surprise.

"OK Fred, we got a ticket, but no fine. He gave me a list of things to be corrected, and he'll be back to see what we've done in a few weeks. This should give us the time we need to get things in order."

Beth was encouraging, but I still wasn't sure where this was going.

She continued, "Fred, I know you've been up against it and have barely had time to settle in. But we need to fix this."

Beth got my respect using the term "we" She wasn't the typical manager looking to throw me under the bus at the first sign of trouble.

"I'll take care of it, Beth."

She answered, "I know you will. Thank you, Fred."

Beth won my respect and loyalty. I vowed to not let her down.

We had gotten off easy. If the agent had gone through the rest of the training records, he would have found many problems. The agent would have forced us to retrain the problem screeners and not allow them to work in the meantime. If that had occurred, we would not have had enough screeners to open the checkpoint. Sandy worked hard to update the records, but it would take time to retrain everyone.

Chapter 12

I'VE GOT THIS

O ur failure of the FAA test and audit hurt, but we had time to fix the remaining problems before the FAA returned. I had a new administrative staff that was competent, loyal, and amusing. Martin with his delightful Jamaican accent, Mike with his British accent, and Sandy with her Florida redneck drawl, all made for interesting conversation.

Sandy could sometimes get a little loud and emotional, but she worked hard and developed an excellent training program. Martin was doing a good job managing the checkpoint but needed some guidance and supervision. He took direction well, but some cultural issues were beyond his comprehension.

Mike could handle almost any situation. He stabilized Sandy and supervised Martin in a friendly, non-confrontational way. There was a little resentment since he was the new guy on the block, but Mike managed it well. With my team in place, I had the luxury of extra time to monitor the checkpoint's operation from a distance. This was the opportunity I needed to cultivate relationships with much needed support elements such as the Sheriff's Department and Airport officials. I had time to check in with Beth daily, attend airport security meetings, and continue building on what we had. I would meet with Sandy, Martin, and Mike most mornings at Starbucks on B Concourse for planning and brainstorming.

Mike suggested we pay a twenty-five dollar bonus to any screener who discovered a gun or passed an FAA test. I told Mike it was a great idea and to make it policy.

Beth thought it was such a good idea that she matched the award. However, after a short time she was forced to withdraw her support. We found so many guns and passed so many FAA tests that it put a hole in her budget.

Martin was eager to help and incredibly loyal, but he needed close supervision. One day, Martin greeted me as I approached the checkpoint.

Martin began, "Oh, boss mon, I just had such a terrible situation."

I listened intently.

"This lady tried to get through the checkpoint with a monkey."

"A monkey?" I repeated.

" Yes, boss mon, a senile monkey."

"A senile monkey," I again repeated.

"Yes, boss mon, she said it was a senile monkey, this lady in a wheelchair."

"She was in a wheelchair?" I continued repeating his words, trying to confirm what I was hearing.

"Yes boss, a blind lady, in a wheelchair with a senile monkey.

"She was blind?"

"Yes boss and she kept saying her monkey was senile."

All I could do was parrot Martin's words and try to understand what the heck he was telling me. It wasn't working.

Martin continued, "I told her I don't care how stupid your monkey is. You cannot take that animal through this checkpoint."

"Boss, I sent her back up to the ticket counter, but she was very upset."

A few moments later, Beth Palmer arrived at the checkpoint,

"Fred, we have a problem. A disabled traveler with a 'Seeing Eye' monkey support animal was denied entry to the concourse, and she has now missed her flight."

A monkey used as a support animal is unusual, so Beth gave us a pass on this one. The concept of a monkey support animal was foreign to Martin, and he heard the term 'Seeing Eye' as "senile". To Martin, senile meant unintelligent or 'stupid.' The miscommunication cost Beth an upgrade to first class on the next flight out for the traveler and a few first-class vouchers to be used any time in her future.

Another time, Martin tested the x-ray screener by secretly placing the hand grenade test item into a passenger's carry-on. For obvious reasons, the FAA strictly forbids placing a test item in a traveler's luggage. The screener failed to detect the item, and Martin informed the screener that she had failed a test. Then, when he went to look for the bag it was gone along with the passenger.

He ran down the concourse but could not locate the bag or passenger. I shudder to think of the consequences that could have occurred if the hand grenade test item had been discovered mid-flight. I feared the worst but never heard a word about it.

Martin also had his good moments. Pilots were required to go through the same security process as passengers. They resented this, but most accepted the process graciously. On one occasion, a pilot's bag was designated for a hand search. The pilot became loud and abusive to the female screener and refused to allow his bag to be searched. I was standing at the checkpoint, observing, and decided to hang back and see how Martin handled the situation.

He went over and calmly apologized to the pilot, "We are just doing our job Captain."

The uniformed pilot continued berating the screener and refusing to have his bag searched. He was causing an unpleasant scene in front of passengers.

Martin said in his distinctive Jamaican accent, "My captain, who is flying the plane today?"

The pilot replied, "I am," with a confused look.

Martin said, "No, no, my captain, you are not flying the plane today, not today, captain."

By this time, I had Beth Palmer on the phone.

"Tell him to report to my office immediately."

The captain's knees buckled slightly when he was informed that Beth Palmer wanted to see him immediately. When he returned after meeting with Beth, he went through all the security procedures without saying a word.

Martin stood over him for the entire process and, upon successful search of his bag, said, "Have a good flight, my captain."

I never saw that pilot again.

The sheriff's deputies were, for the most part, helpful and attentive to the checkpoint when needed. An exception was Deputy Sheriff Harold Korman. A screener observed the unmistakable outline of a pistol on the x-ray machine monitor. Deputy Korman was nearby and was called to the scene.

Following established procedure, Deputy Korman took possession of the bag, asking to whom it belonged.

A man traveling with his wife and son identified the bag as belonging to his son. The deputy searched the bag and found a toy pistol belonging to the young boy. He returned the toy to the bag and advised the man that he could proceed.

Martin had been observing the process and interrupted.

"No, mon, this can not go, it is not allowed," Martin said, retrieving the bag.

An argument ensued, with the deputy insisting the item was not a threat and should be allowed. A chaotic scene erupted between the deputy, Martin, and the passenger. Mike arrived just in time to take charge and confiscate the toy gun. In front of passengers, the deputy had called screeners stupid and said they didn't know what they were doing.

"A toy gun can't hurt anyone," the deputy argued.

When the incident was brought to my attention, I knew I had to act. It was in my best interest to have a good working relationship with all deputies, but Korman had gone too far. The authority of my assistant manager and supervisor had been undermined in an ugly scene that unfolded in the presence of passengers.

This was my opportunity to make a statement that everyone could understand- passenger checkpoints and all related procedures were not answerable to the Department of Airports or the Sheriff's Department.

The passenger checkpoint was under my authority, as stipulated by the Federal Aviation Administration and the up to date three ring notebooks.

I made a copy of the relevant FAA regulation to support my case:

"No replica of a dangerous or prohibited item shall be allowed aboard aircraft."

Captain Jill Chavis was in charge of the Sheriff's Airport Division. She was professional and a credit to her department. We shared a mutual respect, but I had no idea how she might react to my complaint against one of her deputies. She heard me out, observed my reference to the regulation, and thanked me for bringing it to her attention.

I wondered if my complaint had any effect. A few days later, I got my first clue. I was walking down the central corridor; I could see Deputy Korman approaching from the opposite direction. He strolled casually until he noticed me, our eyes locked for an instant. He jerked his head to the right in a desperate attempt to break eye contact, made a right turn, almost losing his balance, and hastily took a staircase to the upper level.

Hmm, I guess Captain Chavis had a word with him.

Beth Palmer, was intelligent, articulate, and attractive, sporting a captivating smile, but there was a serious side to be reckoned with. One day, while waiting outside her office, she was on her feet, dressing down a male employee. While pointing her finger in his face, she was in the middle of a soul-crushing monologue. I couldn't hear a word, but the body language said it all. When the six-foot employee left the office, tears were streaming down his face. Beth saw me sitting in the outer office and immediately went from a stone hard face into that familiar smile.

"Hey Fred, come on in," she said. "Can you imagine a puppy dies in flight and he throws the carcass out behind the cargo building? The owners are devastated. What can I do for you, Fred?"

"We've just passed two FAA tests and we are now under audit."

"Ok, great start, let's see where it goes."

Three weeks after our FAA test failure, two agents returned to see what progress we had made. The agents placed test items in two X-ray machines simultaneously. One was a hand grenade, and the other was a pipe bomb simulated device.

The screeners identified both test objects. We passed this most crucial test with credit to Sandy and her training program. Martin became a little flustered, but Mike was there and immediately shut down the checkpoint and notified the sheriff. At first, the sheriff in the area did not respond appropriately. Fortunately, the FAA agents identified themselves and ended the exercise.

I recognized the FAA agent that failed us on his previous visit and soon found out the second agent was Bob Wallace, his supervisor. Agent Wallace was a professional and someone I got to know and respect. He went to the screeners that discovered the test objects and congratulated each for a job well done. However, we were not yet out of the woods. Bob now wanted to do a complete audit of the checkpoint.

Background checks and training records were thoroughly examined. They were perfect, thanks to Sandy. The regulations in the three-ring notebooks were audited against a master list and were found to be up to date.

Bob asked, "What did you do with the extra test devices you had? There were two extra hand grenades and one extra pipe bomb simulated device identified on the last audit. It is a violation to have extra test items."

I replied cautiously, "I recycled them."

"Ok, good," he said.

I was relieved that this line of questioning did not go any further, as I had a serious problem getting rid of the extra items. Neither the Sheriff's Department nor the Airport wanted anything to do with them. I could not fly them back to corporate, as putting them on an airplane would be a federal violation. Placing them in the garbage could trigger an incident. So, I did the only practical thing available to me. I took them home and threw them into the canal behind my house.

The passenger checkpoint on Concourse C, used by Beta Airlines, was being audited by other agents at the same time. Ogden Security Company was responsible for that checkpoint.

Beth asked Bob, the FAA supervisor,

"How did we do?"

"You passed everything."

He paused. I could tell he was formulating his next words.

"This is the best checkpoint I've seen in my sector."

I breathed a sigh of relief; we had done it.

Bob continued, "But we have big problems on Concourse C."

Bob looked at me and said, "That's not yours too, is it?"

I replied, "No, not yet."

Beth had a big grin on her face.

Peter Colson, GTS Vice President, set up a meeting with Beth and flew in to discuss renewal of the checkpoint contract. As we entered her office, I was confident she was pleased with my accomplishments. But I underestimated Beth. Peter started by telling Beth all the good things GTS Corporation was doing, but she cut him off.

"Peter, if I renew the contract with your firm, do you guarantee that Fred will be the manager for the duration?"

"Yes, Fred will be here and..."

She cut him off again, turning to me. "Fred, USA Airline is expanding our flight service. We will need to move more passengers expeditiously. What will you need to accomplish our expansion?"

"Well, Beth, the equipment is old, obsolete, actually. If a passenger bumps into the magnetometer, it goes out of spec and must be recalibrated. This takes a few minutes a few times a day. Sometimes the X-ray machine screen shuts down and must be rebooted. This will hold up the line for a few minutes. We have two X-ray machines and two magnetometers. We have room for one more X-ray machine and one more magnetometer. If we opt for additional equipment, we'll need to increase our screener hours. If we install new equipment and expand to three portals fully staffed with screeners, we can do twice the volume easily."

Beth turned back to Peter. "Peter, I like what Fred has said. Let's plan on three new x-ray machines, three new magnetometers, and the appropriate staff that Fred suggests." Turning back to me,

"Fred, is there anything else you need?"

"No, Beth, that should do it."

"Ok, Peter, get that to me as soon as possible. I'll review it, and if it looks good, I'll endorse it and forward it to corporate."

As Peter began to talk, Beth cut him off yet again.

"Thank you, gentlemen. I am due for a conference call."

We thanked her and left the office. As we walked back to the checkpoint, Peter turned to me and said,

"I suppose you want a raise."

I didn't answer.

Peter said, "Ok, but not until she signs the contract."

Peter thanked me for my hard work and caught his flight out.

Beth came down to the checkpoint a while later, wearing a devilish grin.

"Did I do right by you, Fred?

"You sure did, Beth."

"Did you get a raise?"

"Yes, I did."

Beth did a fist pump,

"YES!"

I had to smile. The whole meeting was a contrived show by Beth. She diminished my boss, the Vice President, and elevated me, her manager, in a devious way to highlight my role in securing the new contract. As Beth was leaving, she turned and said,

"Fred, my Skycap contract is coming up for renewal. Tell Peter to factor that in."

The next day, I called Peter.

"Say, Peter, if I was to get the USA Airline contract for Skycaps, would that influence the size of my raise?"

Peter replied, "Get the contract, and you can count on it."

"Ok boss, write it up and send it to Beth; we got it."

"You son of a bitch, you set me up.... Good work, Fred."

Armed Deputy Sheriffs patrol the airport and grounds. They respond to the checkpoint whenever dangerous items are discovered. At an airport security meeting I was engaged in conversation with Captain Chavis of the sheriff's Department.

"So you are the Warden," she said.

"Well Captain, I was at one time."

"If you need anything you know where my office is," she said.

I took this as a sign of approval. I wasn't sure if it was my previous employment or my current performance that got me the recognition. I wondered how much they really knew about me.

There was usually a Deputy Sheriff at or near the checkpoint. If not, there was a red phone at each x-ray operator station which was a no dial connection to the Sheriff's substation. The screening staff had no authority to detain anyone or confiscate any items. All enforcement was left to the Sheriff's Deputies. For the most part they were supportive and quick to respond to problems. With improvements made to the checkpoint we gained even greater respect and cooperation from the Sheriff's Office.

Marty was a regular deputy at the checkpoint. He was very friendly and helpful. If I was in the office, he would come in, sit down and chat with me. We became quite friendly, and I would listen to his rants about other deputies and his bosses.

The first time Marty stopped in my office I was stunned as he related his marriage problems to me.

"My wife kicked me out of the house," he said.

"I'm sorry to hear that, Marty."

"Yeah, her boss moved in with her because he doesn't like hotels."

There was a very long silence as I felt there must be a punchline.

"He's from out of town."

Another long silence.

Marty followed that up with "You don't think anything is going on there, do you?"

"No, of course not." He's got to be playing me, I thought to myself. Evidently not.

One day he was telling me about his sidearm, a Sig Sauer 9mm. He said it was special because of the way a bullet was loaded into the chamber.

He said, "Here I'll show you."

With that he drew his sidearm and commenced to remove the magazine and eject the round from the chamber. "Hey Marty, I don't think that's a good idea."

"No problem, watch."

He then removed the slide from the receiver which is a simple takedown procedure and was about to show me the inner workings when his radio crackled.

"Marty, there are people trapped in the east elevator." Marty put the two halves of his gun on my desk and keyed his mic angrily.

"That's Billings' sector call him."

"Marty, Billings is in the elevator," came the reply.

Marty mumbled, "See, he's always finding ways to get out of work."

Marty then began to reassemble his gun but could not get the two parts to line up. He put the slide and magazine in one pocket and the receiver in the other and shuffled off still muttering. He was answering a call with half a gun in each pocket.

One day Marty and I were talking,

"Say, Marty would you happen to know where I can get something notarized?"

"Sure, do you have it with you?"

"Yeah, I have it right here."

Marty keyed his microphone, "Hey Bill, can you come down to the USA checkpoint?"

Marty said, "Bill's a notary, he'll be glad to do it."

A familiar looking Deputy Sheriff arrived a few minutes later.

Marty said, "Hey Bill, Fred has something he needs notarized."

There was an awkward moment while Bill glared at Marty. He then went about the business of notarizing my paperwork. When he had finished, Bill walked over to Marty and put his finger in Marty's chest.

"Don't ever call me to do anything for one of these fucking people again."

Bill walked off and Marty was obviously horrified.

"I'm sorry Fred," Marty said.

"No worries, Marty, I got my papers notarized."

My mind was racing, I wanted to respond in some way but was left to my own thoughts. Bill held the belief that my screeners and I were inferior to him.

Did Bill ever serve his country? Probably not.

"I wore a uniform, too only my shirt was white with crisp pleats and Captain's bars on the collar. That's something a sorry human being like Bill will never see."

I was angry and also disappointed that a person in such an important position could be so arrogant. We were all supposed to work together as a team with the safety of the public our sworn duty. My anger subsided with the realization that Bill was just a small-minded angry man.

There was usually a deputy at the checkpoint but on Monday mornings there could be as many as three. One deputy in particular, Gilbert, was always present on Monday no matter what his sector was.

They were there to watch the show as the exotic ladies in for the weekend were flying back out. Many of them were regulars and would chat with my staff and the deputies. One friendly girl told me she flew in from California every Friday to work the strip clubs and flew out Monday morning.

The Deputies liked the show. Gilbert would make comments and kissing noises in the most inappropriate manner. His behavior was an embarrassment until one of the girls told him to get a blow-up doll. The laughter that followed curtailed his lewd behavior.

Early one Monday morning we had just opened the checkpoint. Martin was at the only open magnetometer. Far down the main corridor we could see our first traveler walking towards the checkpoint. Due to the distance she just appeared to be a spot of red. As she drew closer it was like watching a movie. She was a very attractive young lady in a tight-fitting red dress. The dress contained no more material than a typical bath towel. Her gait was that of a model. Her hips swung so far left then right in an almost gymnastic rhythm. The long necklace she wore swung as much but in the opposing direction.

Her gait did not change as she walked through the magnetometer, all the time looking straight ahead. The alarm sounded and she hesitated for a moment. Martin moved forward with the hand wand, hesitated, and then waved her on with a "Have a nice flight."

Martin then noticed that I was watching. I could see the fear in his face having caught him giving a pass to this woman after an alarm. Then he shrugged his shoulders, raising his arms to the side.

"She had nothing on her boss mon."

No, she did not. That was obvious.

Ogden Security was responsible for the checkpoint at the concourse used by Beta Airlines. Bob, my new FAA friend, said they had serious problems and could not pass a simple simulated weapons test. I met Casey Stone, the Beta Manager at one of the security meetings. He was a gruff, not so friendly, cuss. He had the reputation of being the Big Dog at the airport, sucking up all the attention. He was very opinionated, and no one would go up against him, not even Airport Management.

At one such meeting I approached him. "Hey Casey, do you have a moment?"

"What's up?"

"Well, I've had several of your screeners come down to my checkpoint to apply for a job. I know you have a problem there, so I don't want to hire anyone away from you," he didn't say anything until I added, "And look if there is any way I can help, let me know, no obligation."

He replied, "We're doing ok," and walked off.

My initial impression was that I screwed up with this approach. None of his screeners had approached me for a job and I wasn't sure just how much of a problem existed. At the end of the meeting, he passed by where I was seated and said.

"Have Peter call me."

I called my boss, Peter as soon as I got back to the checkpoint.

"Hey, how do you know Casey?"

"That son of a bitch, yeah, we've done business. Is he giving you any trouble?"

"No, he wants you to call him."

"Ok, sounds like he's interested. I know Beth is happy and word spreads."

Chapter 13

IT WILL ALL WORK OUT

Peter flew in for our meeting with Beta Manager Casey Stone. Beta Airlines was the largest carrier at the airport, and Casey felt that made him the big dog in the neighborhood. He was obnoxious and demanding during our meeting. He said, Beta Airlines would only entertain a contract if it included three new x-ray machines with magnetometers at no cost to Beta.

Among his demands were staffing patterns that would be impossible to manage and not efficient, or economically feasible. It was obvious he was just being a blowhard and had no idea how to efficiently run a passenger checkpoint.

He also wanted assurance that I would be the manager for the duration of the contract. I am sure that Casey and Beth talk, but aside from my management style, I doubt they agree on very much. Beth is an intelligent manager who has everyone's respect. Casey is not only a bully, but he's just proven he's not very smart. I was worried that Peter agreed to some of Casey's outlandish demands.

Peter said "Anything is possible, I'll get you a draft proposal within a week.

As we returned to my office, I asked,

"Do you really think we can meet all those crazy demands?"

Peter said, "Of course not, he's a fucking idiot, we just need his support. He's all bluster; they work these things out at the corporate level. They have a more realistic view of the process."

I added, "We should go after his Sky Cap contract since we're in his favor."

Peter warned, "Don't take on too much at once."

That was good advice, but I was already pushing the limit. The USA Airline security checkpoint was finally operating efficiently with a full compliment. I acquired the USA Airline Skycap account and made critical improvements by appointing a skycap manager and providing much needed training. Unfortunately, I underestimated how hard it would be to maintain my initial success.

The Beta contract was signed and we had a start date of April first. I would have access to the Beta Concourse C checkpoint and employees on that date. The checkpoint, equipment, and all employee training files belong to Ogden Security until the last flight out on March 31st. After the last flight, new X-ray machines and magnetometers would be installed. Installation and calibration could take all night, but everything must be ready for the first flight on April first. April fool's day, what could go wrong.

Screeners would be in the employ of Ogden Security when they went home on March 31st. On April 1st, they would return to be employed by Global Total Services or GTS.

I arrived at the Beta security checkpoint just in time to see workers finishing up installing the new equipment. Sandy arrived with a group of newly trained screeners, and together with the former Ogden screeners, we had enough staff to open all three passenger lanes. I had Mike and Sandy assist with our new Beta operation, leaving Martin to supervise the USA Airline checkpoint.

The Beta Checkpoint did more than twice the volume of the USA Airline checkpoint, and within minutes of opening, we were swamped. The Ogden employees were poorly trained; our new employees had no experience. There were long lines and delays at each portal. I observed one of the Ogden screeners waving passengers through a magnetometer that continuously alarmed. I rushed over to him.

"What are you doing? They have not been cleared."

He replied, "When it gets busy like this, we don't have time to screen them."

I removed the screener and had Mike take over his spot. Sandy was working with the X-ray operators who were not familiar with the new X-ray machines. I was running from one problem to another.

Casey showed up red-faced yelling threats and obscenities.

"You can't have lines like this; you must move them faster. I'll cancel this fucking contract."

We were under pressure to move passengers faster than proper security would allow. After a few moments of panic and self-doubt, I confronted Casey.

"Casey, proper security takes time. This is our first day, and we will get better at it but for now, safety and security are more important than speed."

He stormed off, "I'm calling Peter."

This was bad, but it was going to get worse.

I fired half the Ogden workforce that day, as they were beyond rehabilitation. Many insisted that we needed to understand how things had to be done to get along with Casey. If I fail, it will be because I operate a secure checkpoint. I won't be bullied into half assed work. Although I may be fired.

On our first day, two flights were delayed due to processing times at the checkpoint. Airline Managers are held responsible for the critical on-time departures. Casey's boss would not give any comfort to his excuse that the checkpoint contractor was to blame. This put me on Casey's hit list.

The following day, we only had enough staff to open two passenger lanes, and that was after I borrowed a couple of screeners from the USA Airline checkpoint. This again resulted in long lines and flight delays. I had to get Sandy back to training new employees, and Mike my assistant manager was operating an X-ray machine. As chaos unfolded around me, I saw Beth approaching the Beta checkpoint.

"Fred, there's a big problem. I need to speak with Peter."

I said, "Is there anything I can do?"

She said, "No, Fred, you are the problem."

Peter dropped everything and flew in the next day after receiving calls from Beth and Casey. I was convinced I would be fired.

I said, "Peter, there is no question; we had a chaotic start with Beta Airlines, and we are working on the problem. Sandy is training a new class of screeners. They will be available in a few days. It improves a little each day and I think within a week, or two at the most we should be ok.

"How about Beth?"

"With Beth, I'm not sure. We were doing OK."

Peter was his usual calm self. He seemed concerned but not panicked.

Peter said, "OK, let's go see Beth first. We can work with Beth on whatever the issue is. Casey will be another story."

Beth welcomed us into her office with a straight face and a strict business attitude. The familiar smile was absent.

She began, "Peter, I went to my checkpoint yesterday morning to find Martin, the checkpoint supervisor, working the x-ray machine."

Beth had yet to look me in the eye.

She continued, "Martin told me he was shorthanded, so he had to work a position rather than supervise. I asked him where Fred was, and Martin said everyone was at the Beta Checkpoint, including two of his screeners."

I had second thoughts about leaving Martin alone; his conversation with Beth confirmed that. I should have brought Martin to the Beta checkpoint and left Mike to manage the USA Airline checkpoint.

Peter said, "Beth, we had a rough couple of days, but we should be back on track soon."

Beth replied, "That's not good enough. You assured me that Fred would manage my checkpoint, and now he is at Beta Airlines, along with his assistant manager and two of my screeners. You have gone back on your word."

Peter was on the hot seat along with me. This debate went back and forth for a while. Beth charged that she was paying for my services while I was working at the Beta checkpoint. Peter explained that she only paid for the hours worked by screeners at her checkpoint.

"Fred's job is to oversee all GTS business at the Airport, including Beta Airlines and USA Airlines. Screeners might shift back and forth between checkpoints but you are only billed for actual hours at your checkpoint."

Beth directed all of her comments at Peter. They did not invite me into the conversation.

Beth was not satisfied, but the meeting ended amicably, with Peter pledging continued attention to her needs.

Her final warning was, "I understand your desire to expand your business at this airport, but do not do so at the expense of USA Airlines."

Peter said to me on the way out, "OK, that went well; let's go see Casey."

Beth was measured and professional in her dissatisfaction. She also had an excellent point. I felt I had let her down, and I promised myself I would make up for it and hopefully regain her trust.

Casey, on the other hand, lived up to his reputation as a bully. He ranted and raved, sparing no curse word for the first five minutes of our meeting. He summed up his frustration by pounding his desk and declaring,

"I will cancel this fucking contract."

Peter stared back at Casey and said,

"I can have my people out of here in twenty minutes; just say the word."

They just glared at each other. Peter waited a long time for a response.

Then, continued when there was none.

"We took over from a company that was a total failure. We inherited employees that could not do the job. We must train and hire new staff. We will not take shortcuts like Ogden Security did. We will build trust and credibility with the FAA. Fred knows what he is doing; you must give him the time to do it."

Peter had sucked the oxygen out of the room. There wasn't much left to say. Casey agreed to wait and see how things developed, and we parted with handshakes.

His parting words were directed at Peter: "This better get fixed quick."

As we left, Peter said, "OK, now you can go after his Sky Cap contract."

After our meetings, Peter and I hung out at Starbucks, waiting for his flight. I got the sense he did this in a different airport every day. GTS Global Total Services was a large corporation that provides airline services worldwide. Peter was the vice president in charge of the Southeast United States.

I didn't get fired; I didn't even get chewed out. I was upset that Casey, and especially Beth, felt I was not doing a good job. Peter sensed that I was stressed out and feeling responsible for our poor performance. Peter was good at his job and needed to get me back on track. Nothing seemed to phase him. I admired Peter for calling Casey's bluff when he threatened to cancel the contract.

Peter said, "Fred we expanded fast in Palm Beach. I don't know of anyone who could have accomplished what you have. All I can tell you is keep doing what you're doing, and it will all work out."

After Peter left, I met with Mike, Sandy and Martin. Peter flying in and our meeting with Beth and Casey had them really shaken. I let them know that Peter and I appreciated their hard work and the results they had achieved. I spoke to them as a group and complimented each of them on specific accomplishments. I could sense the loyalty each of them had toward me and our company. I gave them the same advice Peter had given me.

"Just keep doing what you are doing, and it will all work out."

Over the next couple of weeks, we climbed out of the hole we were in. We caught up on training, record keeping and had sufficient staff to operate both checkpoints. Beth seemed cautiously pleased with the operation.

Casey could be seen observing the checkpoint from a distance daily without complaint. I opened the third lane for one hour in the morning and one hour in the afternoon by shifting staff between checkpoints and occasionally assigning Mike and Sandy as screeners.

Months went by, and I hadn't pissed anyone off. I guess I was overdue. Two incidents in a row got the Department of Airports and the Airport Director, Catherine Holiday up in arms.

One evening, I was observing the USA Airline checkpoint. There was little traffic, and I was about to go play some pool when a man appeared, pushing a large cart. The supervisor cleared the man through the magnetometer and then was about to allow him to take his cart through the passenger exit lane without inspection. I intervened and told the supervisor that the cart had to be inspected.

The man was a telephone company employee, and the cart contained hundreds of payphone coin boxes. The year was probably 1996 when hundreds of pay telephones were at the airport. The airport realized substantial revenue in an arrangement with the phone company.

The coin boxes were made of metal and about six inches square. I advised the telephone company employee that he would have to open each box for inspection.

He stated, "The boxes can't be opened; I don't have a key." I take a full coin box from the pay phone and replace it with an empty one."

I said, "They can only go through the checkpoint if inspected."

I realized the difficulty involved in my demand and expected blowback, but I was following FAA regulations.

After a few phone calls, a Department of Airports supervisor showed up. After some discussion, I retrieved the hand grenade test item and held it alongside one of the boxes as a demonstration.

"You have to prove to me that a real one is not hidden inside a coin box."

The airport supervisor said, "You have to use common sense."

"Actually," I replied, "I am not permitted to use common sense."

I knew I was on solid ground, denying the coin boxes to pass. I also knew I was going to piss a lot of people off. My actions started a war between the phone company and airport management.

The airport director, Catherine Holiday, threatened to overrule me or have me fired. They solved the problem temporarily by bringing the coin boxes onto the tarmac and then carrying them up the stairs to the concourse, thus circumventing the checkpoint. It accomplished their objective but was a tremendous burden for the phone company. The phone company threatened to remove all payphones from the airport.

That problem was still being debated when I pissed them off again. Some vendor spaces on the Beta concourse were scheduled for renovation. One morning without notice a construction crew showed up at the Beta checkpoint with boxes of tools. The workers wanted to go through the checkpoint with power tools, screw drivers, hammers and other items banned by FAA regulations. The workers hung around most of the day while their case was debated, and I was again threatened.

Catherin Holiday the airport director, would have no more of me and called for a meeting of all interested parties, including the FAA. I called Peter to let him know the meeting was scheduled and that the airport director was after my scalp.

Peter asked, "Are you on solid ground with this?"

I replied, "Yes, I am."

"Then you handle it; you have my full authority to act in my place. I'm tied up with another issue."

I arrived at the airport conference room for the meeting to find a large group had gathered. Casey was there, along with Beth. Catherin Holiday, the airport director, sat at the head of the table. As I took my place, Bob, the FAA agent I had come to know, entered with a woman I assumed was his boss. Several other participants, whom I did not know filled the remaining chairs. Interested parties were there to witness my hanging. I had a very lonely feeling. As usual it was me against everyone else.

Catherin Holiday began the meeting. "Let's go around the table and introduce ourselves. I took note as each spoke up. I introduced myself with a squeaky, shaky voice.

Bob's boss was the FAA regional director; some other unknowns were airport officials and vendors involved with the renovations.

Holiday spoke first, "The Department of Airports has several issues with the contracting company, GTS. I have invited the FAA here today to address these issues. I would like to hear from some of you first. Beth, would you like to begin? What problems have you had with GTS?"

Ms. Holiday was looking for people to throw me under the bus.

Beth said, "We have had a contentious relationship with GTS due to some problems. However, Mr. Kenney has been quick to address issues efficiently. He runs a very tight checkpoint, which sometimes can seem extreme. But we can all agree that safety is of utmost importance. Whatever problems we had with GTS have been resolved."

Casey was next,

"We had a lot of problems at startup, most of which have been addressed. Mr. Kenney takes security to extremes, so I am glad to see the FAA represented here. We need to get an understanding of the role Mr. Kenney and GTS play in the operation of this airport."

I could see that Holiday wasn't pleased with the comments so far, but she was saving the big guns for last.

"I'd like an assessment from the FAA on GTS checkpoint performance and a determination on the Department of Airports letter of complaint against GTS.

She sent a letter of complaint to the FAA. I had never even met this woman.

Bob began, "We have no issues with the checkpoints for USA Airlines and Beta Airlines. We did have some outstanding issues regarding training records and test failures, but those issues have been resolved."

So far, I wasn't doing too bad.

Holiday had to dig deeper into the failures. "How many test failures has GTS had since they started here?"

Bob checked his records: "The pass rate for this Airports checkpoints under GTS is 85%. I don't have the actual number of failures."

Holiday pushed further, "How does this compare to contractors in other airports."

Bob continued "The pass rate for the former Ogden security at Beta concourse in this airport was 26%.

Holiday and Casey were visibly shaken at this statistic."

Bob wasn't finished, "In my area which is the Southeast other airports run between 30% and 50% pass rate. This airport under GTS has the highest pass rate in my district.

Then, the FAA Director chimed in. "Ms. Holiday, I have your complaint letter addressed to my office regarding the refusal of GTS to allow certain persons and items to bypass security. We have no issue with the actions of GTS or the checkpoint manager. His actions comply with FAA rules and regulations. However, if you wish to take issue with these rules, you may submit a written request for a variance."

There was no place for Holiday to go. I sat stoically with no expression of glee or fist pumping. I was never called upon for a comment, and I'm sure half the participants didn't even know who I was.

Ms. Holiday tried to minimize her defeat by steering the meeting off in a different direction. She made a few program announcements, asked for any new business, and adjourned the meeting.

The Department of Airports figured out how to get the coin boxes and the construction materials where they needed to be without going through the checkpoints. That was fine with me. By January 2001, in addition to contracts for all of the checkpoints at this International Airport, I also had all the Skycap contracts and the plane cleaning contract for Beta Airlines. Altogether, I had about two hundred employees at the airport. Not bad since I started with 20.

Sandy, Martin and especially Mike needed very little input from me. I was working a few hours a day just to touch base with the airline managers and checking in with Mike. I was playing pool most afternoons.

I called Peter, "Peter, I'm going to wind it down. After seven years with GTS, I'm going to resign as of May 1, 2001."

I was giving him almost five months' notice. I sensed his disappointment, but he didn't try to talk me out of it. I told Peter that Mike was more than capable of taking over my position. Eventually, Mike would take a position with the Department of Airports as Manager of Air Cargo. Mike was overqualified for any position at the airport.

My greatest disappointment was that I could not institute the changes that I knew would improve security. I ensured that all FAA rules and regulations were strictly followed but they were not enough. The FAA allowed knives and box cutters onto planes against my better judgement. Too much was allowed in passenger carry-on bags, and they were way too large for proper inspection. The Xray image was a jumble of objects too complex to identify items consistently.

The FAA rule on testing was to put the test item in an empty bag. If a screener missed it, they weren't looking at the screen. It was not a real-world test. The only way to achieve real airline security was to limit the number and size of items allowed through the checkpoint. Airlines were heavy on customer satisfaction and on-time departures. Security was a necessary burden for which we eventually paid a heavy price. Having said that, I want to be clear about my relationship with the airlines. None of the airlines involved ever asked me to sacrifice security to move passengers. Complaints had to do with efficiency, not security. The Federal Aviation Administration made the rules that the Airlines and Security Contractors had to follow. In my seven years at Palm Beach International Airport, we all followed the rules.

I caught many violations by watching the people in line before they entered the checkpoint. Acting nervously and making head and eye movements can often predict nefarious intentions. This is considered profiling and at the time was prohibited.

One day close to my retirement day and not much before the disaster of 911, Mike and I were watching a busy Beta Checkpoint. I noticed a man about ten people back in line who caught my attention. He was acting nervously and looking in various directions. At times, he would turn completely around, looking behind him.

I told Mike to go over and personally attend to him when he came through the metal detector. The man had no carry-on bag but alarmed the metal detector upon walking through it. Mike stepped up with the hand wand, telling the man to raise his arms. The man whirled about and ran back the way he had come, running up the down escalator to the third level, which was the drop-off level. I alerted a nearby deputy sheriff, pointing the man out to him as he ran up the down escalator. The Deputy shrugged his shoulders and stated,

"He's going in the right direction. He's leaving, so it's not my problem."

That summed up the mindset of airline security before 911.

The fleeing man discarded his jacket as he got to the third level, ran to the curb, and entered a waiting vehicle. They sped off, never to be identified.

I have no doubt this was a nefarious test of the checkpoint with a planned escape route in the event of failure. Could this have been one of the 911 hijackers? I personally feel it is highly likely. Although there was an incident report filed to my knowledge there was no further follow-up. It is only my opinion, but it is likely Palm Beach Airport was tested by the 911 hijackers who felt security was too tight for their purposes. I left my position four months before the tragic events of 911.

On September 1, 2001, I was at home watching TV with my mother when the first plane hit the tower. It was horrible, but when the second plane hit, I jumped up and yelled

"Shut it down, Shut it down."

My mother said, "You want me to shut the TV off."

"No, they need to shut down all air traffic, we're under attack."

I had a limited role in Airport Security but, I wish I could have done more. When I left Palm Beach International Airport it was one of the safest for passengers in the country. That was not my assessment but that of the FAA regional director.

Chapter 14

BRINGING MOM

I was once again retired, and this time for good. I was still young and fit. My pool game was better than ever. All the drama was gone from my life and I no longer had other people's problems to solve. It felt good to have nothing to do except play pool and fish. I was only a couple of weeks into retirement, and I was content.

Early on a Monday morning, the phone rang. It was my mother's neighbor, Georgia. My mother lived on the fourth floor of an apartment in Mount Vernon, New York. She was a young 85-year-old who was out and about every day. She did not drive, but she had many well-to-do friends happy to take her places for mutual enjoyment. I spoke to my mother every few days and had just spoken to her. She sounded her usual chipper self and assured me that all was well.

Georgia relayed a contrary set of facts. My mother had not been out of her apartment in weeks. She was not eating and could not walk. She seemed to be wasting away. My first thought was to fly to New York and tend to her needs. Thinking it through, I would lack the resources so far from home to be effective. Georgia suggested that if I were to fly to New York, she would meet me at the airport with Mom. I arranged to fly to New York and return on the same flight with my mother.

Georgia met me at the gate with my mother in a wheelchair. Mom looked awful and was very feeble. I had to carry her onto the aircraft for the return flight to Florida.

I was going to have a quiet day and maybe go fishing. Instead, I had been to New York and back, and Mom was living with me. Mom was not in good shape and I was afraid to leave her alone. First, I had to take care of her short-term needs before considering future living conditions.

The next day, after making Mom comfortable in the spare bedroom, I set out to get needed supplies. There was a medical supply store in West Palm Beach that I had passed by many times. I needed a wheelchair to get Mom around and some bed and bath equipment to make life easier for her.

As I pulled into a parking space by the entrance, a van pulled in alongside me. It was painted primer grey with stickers covering most of the exterior. Most of the stickers were Vietnam Veteran related, patriotic flags and silly bumper stickers. As I exited my vehicle, I could see the driver standing behind his van. Thinking nothing of it I proceeded toward the front door when I heard.

"Hey, buddy can you give me a hand?"

I looked to see the man marching in place. He was a big man, obviously a Vietnam veteran by way of the patch covered vest he wore. He had a bushy beard and hair down past his shoulders.

I walked over to him, "What can I do for you." as he continued to march in place, first lifting his left foot then right but not advancing.

"Get behind me and give me a shove."

Somewhat perplexed I got behind him and gave him a little push.

"No, he said, "Give me a good shove."

Fearing the worst I gave him a firm shove and off he went marching into the store. As he went, he waived his right hand in the air, exclaiming,

"Thank you, buddy."

Georgia had been smart enough to pack Mom's medications, and I brought them when I took Mom to see my doctor. I've been going to this doctor for years and he's the nicest guy you will ever meet. After a quick examination, he asked mom how she felt mentally.

Her response was. "Do you know how you feel when you first realize you lost your wallet?"

"Yes," he replied.

Mom said, "Well, I feel like that all the time."

I've lost a wallet a time or two in my lifetime. That first "Oh Shit" moment is powerful. Her explanation impressed me and the doctor. He referred Mom to a psychiatrist and doubled up on some of her meds. He also gave me the name of a hematologist who I might consider if all else failed.

The psychiatrist we settled on was a young woman who seemed very nice. She asked Mom a lot of questions.

"What is today's date? Who is the president? What is your address?" Mom got most of these wrong, but that did not surprise me. She lived a simple life and did not read the newspaper or get involved in politics. She did not need to know what the date was. I had not told her my address. The doctor prescribed Alzheimer's medication and scheduled a future visit.

Mom said, "I'm not going back to her, I don't like her."

"She seemed very nice, why don't you like her."

Mom said, "Because she gave me Alzheimer's."

I didn't feel we were getting anywhere, and with every new doctor, mom's medication list grew. I decided to try the hematologist suggested by my doctor. The appointment was a month out and I was cautioned to bring all medications and available medical records. With plenty of time, I acquired her extensive medical records from New York and the doctors I had taken her to in Florida.

The day finally arrived for her visit to the hematologist, who was highly regarded. The doctor did a quick examination of my mother and then spent the next half hour pondering her medical records. finally, I interrupted him and said,

"She is on a lot of medications, and I am concerned."

The doctor looked up, smiled, and said, "You should be a doctor; you're spot on."

I looked at him quizzically "What?"

The doctor said, "Stop all of her medications; your mother will be fine."

A few weeks later, Mom was up and about, clear-headed, physically regaining strength, and taking no meds.

I could not let her return to New York, so I flew up and engaged a realtor to sell her condominium. With Georgia's help, I cleared out the apartment. Mom insisted her dining room table, chairs, and personal items be packed and brought to Florida. I hired a moving company, and her furniture was placed in a local storage. I owed Geogia a great debt, which I paid by giving her several nice pieces of furniture.

Mom had a few great years after initially getting her strength back. She wanted to get her own apartment, and we looked at a few places. I didn't think it was a good idea, so we usually found a couple of reasons why each location wasn't right. She pitched in around the house and was always cleaning or trying to help.

This memoir, from the beginning, has never been about family, and that won't change in this chapter. These events are not about my mother but the effect this period of my life had on me. At my mother's best times, I was in my worst depression. When her health began to fail for the last time, I was barely able to function. I had no help in dealing with the ups and downs of caring for Mom. Her presence in my home caused a great deal of acrimony that I constantly had to absorb for both of us. I did that willingly because it was the right thing to do.

I was pleased that I had recaptured a few good years for mom. She would say to me,

"Freddie, can we go visit my furniture today?"

"Sure Mom."

We would drive to the storage facility where her dining room table and chairs were stored, and she would make sure everything was OK. I stored that dining room set for five years at one hundred dollars a month. After mom passed I sold the set for one hundred and fifty dollars.

Mom didn't need the wheelchair any longer, but I got her a walker to make me feel better. Mom said,

"I can't let people see me with that."

Mom loved to shop; she was an expert on ladies' clothing since she had worked for some of the most exclusive dress shops in New York. She worked as a commissioned salesperson, buyer, and, at times, a model. For a time, she worked in the exclusive lady's dress department of Bergdorf Goodman. She was a successful salesperson but not tech-savvy on using the sales computer. The other salespersons and department manager complained about her holding everyone up while attempting to use the register. Her supervisor complained to the store manager and wanted my mother to be fired.

The store manager met with all the sales staff and the department manager.

He said, "I know Eleanor is having a little trouble with the register. I am sure, given time, she will learn to use it properly. In the meantime, if she has any trouble, you do it for her because she outsells all of you put together."

Mom, had a book of very wealthy clients who followed her from store to store. She made friends with people, customers, and strangers instantly.

Mom loved to shop at a nearby mall while living with me. I would drive her to the mall and drop her off at a side entrance. We chose that entrance because a bench was conveniently located by the door. We decided when I would pick her up and she could sit on the bench if she arrived early. After the first couple of times, she decided to use the walker.

"What time should I pick you up?"

"Come back in four hours Freddie."

"Mom, that's too long."

"OK make it three hours."

When I returned, she would be sitting on the bench talking to a new friend. Sometimes I would have to wait five or ten minutes for them to finish their conversation.

"Such a nice lady," she would say, "Her husband passed away three years ago, and she lives with her son now."

Mom would have a few packages that she purchased. She would purchase items one day and return them the next. Purchase, return, repeat was the drumbeat.

Mom's health began to decline again after the few years that we managed to salvage. She continually fought and clawed her way back from poor health, but at ninety, it was a difficult battle. Even when she fell and broke her hip at ninety years of age, she was able to bounce back briefly.

Mom lay in a hospital bed for three days with a broken hip before surgery could be scheduled. Mom would not let me leave her alone. I stayed with her sneaking out at night for a few hours after she was medicated and asleep. In the morning, after she awakened, she would quiz me sternly.

"You didn't leave while I was sleeping, did you?"

"No, Mom, of course not."

I finally met the surgeon who was to perform the surgery.

"Doc, can she survive surgery at her advanced age."

He looked at me impassively and said, "Some do, some don't."

I wondered if he would be this indifferent about getting paid.

Mom went to thirty days of rehab straight from the hospital but was very unhappy and cried a lot begging me to take her home. She would not cooperate with her rehabilitation schedule. Citing Medicare rules Mom was ordered discharged before her entitled 30 days of rehab. While she was in rehab, I was putting in more time than a full-time nurse. I could sneak home at night when she was sleeping or during the day when she was in a class. Now, at home, I was again on duty 24 hours a day.

This had been going on for months. I was exhausted and stressed with no end in site. Mom bounced back again and had some good days. However, that did not last long and she returned to the hospital. The doctor came to me and said.

"Your Mom's not sick, we all have a life cycle, and your mom is at the end of hers. Would you like to speak with someone from hospice?"

This was not an easy decision, but I agreed to talk with someone.

I met two ladies in the cafeteria. Upon sitting down at the table with them I lost it and began to cry uncontrollably. I wasn't distraught about my mother's condition; I could accept that. I was just physically and emotionally exhausted. At that point, I think the ladies decided they needed to save me.

Hospice of Palm Beach took over relieving me of that awful burden. They outfitted Mom's room at home with a hospital bed, oxygen, and medical supplies to make her comfortable. Mom arrived home by private ambulance. She was alert and so happy to be home. A nurse and a doctor accompanied her. The doctor advised me that my mother would receive nursing care around the clock.

I asked, "How long will you do this."

He answered, "Until your mother gets well, or until she passes away."

Nurses worked in shifts twenty-four hours a day. They fixed Mom's hair, bathed her, and ensured her comfort. They tended to her so gently and sweetly. I have never met such caring people. Betty, the regular daytime nurse, would say to me, "Go to a movie or get out of the house and go for a drive. This organization, with these wonderful people, saved my life. Mom was no longer dependent solely on me. I could appreciate my time with her without worrying about what I had to do next. Almost two weeks after mom arrived home, she passed away. She died peacefully without pain as I held her hand and said,

"I'm ok mom, you can go, don't worry, I'll be ok."

There was no funeral or service. I was the only one to care. I had Mom's ashes and planned to take them to New York to be placed with her mother.

I cleaned out the storage and sold Mom's furniture. No profit was made since I had paid storage for five years. I went through the boxes discarding most of the contents. Two bundles of letters got my attention. The first bundle contained every letter I had sent to my mother while I was in the Navy. Reading about my thoughts and adventures of so long ago was interesting. So many things I had completely forgotten about. I never wrote to her about the fears and horrors of war that I faced. Just the fun stuff and the assurance at the end of every letter that I was ok.

The second bundle was the find of a lifetime. Dozens of letters from my father to my mother. I organized the letters by date, studying each intently, hopeful for what they might reveal.

From the time my father failed to show up when I was five through my life till now, I have searched for answers. I had questioned everyone that may have known him. There was a reluctance to talk about him.

People would claim ignorance. My Mom would not speak of him at all and if I pressed, she would get upset and cry. The hurt must have been unimaginable.

With mom gone there was no one left to query. The letters were a treasure trove or a path to an even deeper mystery, never to be fully resolved. I had over time found out a few things about my father. He was trained as an optician. He was best friends with my Uncle Harold who would not speak of him. He was born in County Waterford Ireland to parents who were US citizens. They were visiting relatives in Ireland at the time of his birth. He was born in Ireland as a dual citizen.

He died in 1992 and I discovered this by searching the Social Security Death index. That information led me to obtain a death certificate from California. A woman's name appeared on the death certificate as a contact person.

I was able to contact her, and she related some interesting facts. Before retiring my father worked for a large firm as an Optician. He mentored this woman Alison, as an optician at the firm. He was also helpful to her after a tragic auto accident left her a paraplegic. She said my father had been married five times. My uncle Harold once told me that my father had one big problem, "He loved the ladies."

Alison said my father had two other children besides me who he was estranged from. Alison said that when my father became ill with colon cancer she was helpful in getting him into hospice. She said she had all of his furniture and belongings in a spare room.

Alison had to go, and I asked if I could call again. She said yes but I would have to call between 2AM and 3AM. Due to her infirmity she slept during the day and was awake after midnight. On the next call Allison was not as forthcoming and expressed annoyance at my questions. I had asked her if she had a piece of his jewelry or something personal of his she could have sent to me. I got the impression she was concerned about me wanting his property.

I was hoping to acquire something to help me feel close to him. I was looking for some closure. Soon after the first call she severed all contact. I knew there was a lot more to this story but like so many other situations I would never know.

I began sorting the letters by date hoping to unveil a chronicled screen play. Some letters were not dated, and some pages were missing. Most all letters were love letters. He went on paragraph after paragraph, longing to hold her, kiss her, be with her. Every once in a while there would be a clue to his activities. Instead of answering all my questions countless new mysteries were created. I could not help but feel my mother had done me a great disservice by hiding so much.

The first letter from my father to my mother was dated April 24, 1934, he was 22 years old and I was not yet born. My future father was on his way to Ireland on the SS Manhattan. The letter recapped the reason for his travel. His grandfather had left him 200 acres on the Irish coast near Dungarvin. He was on his way to claim his inheritance. Much of the letter was a love letter. He went on for some time on how it was so difficult to leave her the night before. He was, however, happy she did not come to the pier to see him off as that would be heartbreaking.

I remember when I was sixteen in order to get a job, I had to apply for working papers and produce a birth certificate. I went to City Hall and gave the clerk my name and date of birth. She came back shortly with a birth certificate that said

"Mother: Eleanor Murphy"

I said, "No this is not mine; my mother is Eleanor Kenney."

The clerk said, "It is probably her maiden name."

I again said, "No, her maiden name is Colbert."

The clerk said, "Go home and talk to your mother kid."

It turned out my grandmother had remarried and maybe my mother was unmarried when I was born. I don't know for sure.

I pieced together a little information about my father's trip to Ireland. He wrote about two dozen letters over a two-month period. My fathers mother accompanied him, and they stayed with his mother's sister for awhile. My father reconnected with a cousin while there. They went rabbit hunting on horseback with greyhound dogs. My father was thrown from his horse and received a slight injury. While being treated he told the doctor about his inheritance. The doctor said he would be interested in purchasing a few acres.

My father took the doctor to see the property and described a beautiful beach overlooking the ocean. There was a working lighthouse on the property that he said was being retained by the local government. The property was currently being surveyed and he had not yet received ownership. He had several other offers for portions of the property, but he could take no action.

I went on Google Earth and found the only lighthouse near Dungarvin. It was built in the 1800's and there is a beautiful sandy beach beside it. My father's property is now a golf course.

He wrote about going to London on business which must have had something to do with the property. One letter spoke of disappointment.

"There were taxes on the property and the tenants had not paid rent in years."

After two months in Ireland, he was boarding a ship for home his purse the poorer for his trip according to one letter. To realize the full potential of his inheritance, he would have to remain in Ireland for several more months. He was not willing to do that but also stated he could not stay if he wanted to. His mother remained in Ireland at least for the time being.

He had been in Ireland from April 1934 until June 1934. He was happy to be going home and the prospect of seeing the one he loved. I have no idea what may have happened to two hundred acres of oceanfront property, but the letters now took an unexpected turn.

The next letter was dated February 1935 and it described how he left my mother and New York and was on his way to Texas to find work. All the letters to this date were signed "All my love Freddie". The next letter dated March 1935 described his arrival in Texas and it was signed "All my love, Toni". The next 30 letters describing various jobs and living conditions in Texas were signed "All my love Toni". At first, I thought this must be a different person, but the handwriting and overall appearance were the same. The letters instead of solving a mystery, created a greater mystery that I must live with. I am left with more questions than answers. Why did his name change to Toni.

This memoir contains names of those who impacted my life. The one person I so missed was my father. I searched for him my entire life. I needed answers and closure that have remained elusive. I could understand him leaving my mother. She was no bargain when I was young. I cannot understand how a man can walk away from his son and not even look back. I needed answers that would never come.

He gave me no direction, but he did influence me. I would not be like him. Given choices I would always do the right thing. I never asked myself, "What is the best thing or safest thing to do. My intention was always the same, "What is the right thing to do." It always worked out. This is not the end, my journey continues.

A PAIL OF BEER

Epilogue

If you have reached this point in my memoir, I thank you, the reader, for taking the time to be a part of my journey. I would love to hear from you. You may contact me at frederickkenney.com or email at Fred@floridafred.com or pailofbeer.com

You can help me tell my story by leaving a REVIEW on Amazon.com. It would be very helpful and greatly appreciated.

My next project will capitalize on what I have learned from writing "A Pail of Beer" and will be a deep dive into one aspect of the book. Please stay in touch to learn more.

Almost four years on the flight deck of an aircraft carrier was covered in a mere few pages in my book. The true impact of that time emerged gradually over a long period of time. While I experienced PTSD for years, the symptoms of exposure to agent orange and the debilitating noise levels on the flight deck remained dormant.

Over time I began to experience a gradual loss of hearing and a less than gradual degradation of eyesight. I found myself unable to understand casual conversation even with hearing aids. Almost blind in one eye (possibly like Popeye) and seriously impaired in the other my PTSD took on a new vigor.

There is always a way around the obstacles in your life.

My book chronicles how so many people impacted my life and how I was able to overcome and conquer obstacles. This is but one more chapter I have navigated successfully. I must give credit to two more "lives" that have impacted my journey. The first is my wife liz who receives far too little credit. The second is my constant companion and service dog "Gibbs". Just, keep doing what you are doing and it will all work out.